JOHN BUNYAN

ROGER SHARROCK

PROFESSOR OF ENGLISH IN
THE UNIVERSITY OF DURHAM

MACMILLAN
London · Melbourne · Toronto
ST MARTIN'S PRESS
New York
1968

First published by Hutchinson 1954
Reissued by Macmillan 1968

MACMILLAN & CO LTD
Little Essex Street London W C 2
and also at Bombay Calcutta and Madras
Macmillan South Africa (Publishers) Pty Ltd Johannesburg
The Macmillan Company of Australia Pty Ltd Melbourne
The Macmillan Company of Canada Ltd Toronto
St Martin's Press Inc New York

Library of Congress catalog card no. 68-22423

Printed in Great Britain by
Lowe & Brydone (Printers) Ltd., London

CONTENTS

century. He was loyal to his origins because he remained close
to them. With the exception of preaching excursions to London
in his later days, he spent his whole life in Bedford and its
neighbourhood. The sixty years of his life bridge the Civil
Wars, in which he played his minor part as conscript in a county
levy, and the Puritan Revolution. His career as a sectarian
preacher continued, in and out of prison, throughout the heroic
age of Nonconformity under Charles II, and ended within a
few days of the Revolution of 1688, which put an end to the
ruggle by incorporating the sects in the national

a part of the militant phase
sistance und

PREFACE TO THE 1968 REISSUE

As well as making a few corrections in the text, I have taken
the opportunity to revise and enlarge the bibliography.

Durham, 1967

PREFACE TO THE FIRST EDITION

THE following chapters are intended to furnish a general
introduction to Bunyan's work which incorporates the findings
of modern scholarship; I have tried to do equal justice to his
individual spiritual history and to his place in the Puritan
literary tradition.

In the forefront of my obligations comes a debt to the late
Dr. F. E. Hutchinson, who criticized and encouraged my earliest
work on Bunyan. My thanks are also due to Professor B. A.
Wright and the Rev. Hubert Hoskins who read portions of the
typescript and made valuable suggestions. The Editor of the
Review of English Studies has kindly allowed me to make use of
material originally published in that journal. Among many who
have helped me with information or advice I must mention
Mr. C. S. Lewis; Dr. G. F. Nuttall; Dr. E. A. Payne; Mr.
Owen Watkins; and finally, Professor Basil Willey for his more
than editorial helpfulness and patience.

Southampton, 1954

CHAPTER I

PURITAN ENGLAND

I

JOHN BUNYAN was born in 1628 in the heart of the English Midlands, the son of Thomas Bunyan, a brazier His birthplace was Elstow near Bedf 30th November in the same Registers of the

...dford, and his baptism on
... year is recorded in the Transcript
... Archdeaconry of Bedford. He speaks in his
autobiography of his father's family as "being of that Rank that is
meanest and most despised of all the Families in the Land".
Here his humility makes him exaggerate: the trade of a travelling
tinker certainly had some disreputable exponents in the
seventeenth century, like Shakespeare's Christopher Sly a
generation earlier; to practise it, a licence was required from
two justices of the peace, which put the tinker on a level with
bear-wards and pedlars. But Bunyan's father was no vagabond;
he had his own cottage in Elstow on which he paid hearth-tax,
and there had been Bunyans owning land in the district for
three hundred years. Documentary evidence of recurring
sales of the family's lands during the sixteenth century indicate
that the Bunyans were at that period yeomen farmers who
were going down in the world. However, they did not yet
belong to the very poor. When Thomas Bunyan's father, who
described himself as a "Pettie Chapman", died in 1641, he had
some property to dispose of and had made a will.

Bunyan is the greatest representative of the common
people to find a place in English literature. English social
distinctions have never been rigid, and many small yeoman's
sons in that age rose by grammar school and university to
distinguish themselves in letters or the public service. But
Bunyan's voice remains that of the popular culture of rural
England, preserved much as it had been in the middle ages
until it was swept away by the enclosures of the following

Thus Bunyan's life story is also p   of English Puritanism, and of its heroic re   under persecution. *The Pilgrim's Progress* is one of the chief channels by which the Puritan spirit has entered the main stream of the English tradition. However, Bunyan did not live his whole life within the bounds of Nonconformist orthodoxy, and in this respect he is unlike other outstanding Puritan figures of the seventeenth century; both George Fox and Richard Baxter came of "godly" parents. He grew up as a typical member of a village community, not marked off from his fellows by any special pretensions to piety. The Puritanism of his life and his books retains much of this larger background: it owes most to the immensely diffused influence of the English Bible, and to the sturdy evangelical Christianity native to the eastern and east Midland counties. The extreme sectaries and fanatics came and went, but in the course of the seventeenth century this moderate Puritan ethos gradually permeated whole sections of the artisan and middle classes.

In Bunyan's age, the social and economic, as well as the religious life of the village, still revolved around the parish church. Conformity with its worship, signified by attendance at church on Sunday, was the essential badge, not merely of religious orthodoxy, but of participation in community life. Absence from church entailed a shilling fine levied under the warrant of a justice. If the absences continued, the offenders could be presented at the Archdeacon's court by the church-wardens. If, from one aspect, the state control of the church after the Elizabethan settlement might seem to secularize

PURITAN ENGLAND

I

JOHN BUNYAN was born in 1628 in the heart of the English Midlands, the son of Thomas Bunyan, a brazier or tinker. His birthplace was Elstow near Bedford, and his baptism on 30th November in the same year is recorded in the Transcript Registers of the Archdeaconry of Bedford. He speaks in his autobiography of his father's family as "being of that Rank that is meanest and most despised of all the Families in the Land". Here his humility makes him exaggerate: the trade of a travelling tinker certainly had some disreputable exponents in the seventeenth century, like Shakespeare's Christopher Sly a generation earlier; to practise it, a licence was required from two justices of the peace, which put the tinker on a level with bear-wards and pedlars. But Bunyan's father was no vagabond; he had his own cottage in Elstow on which he paid hearth-tax, and there had been Bunyans owning land in the district for three hundred years. Documentary evidence of recurring sales of the family's lands during the sixteenth century indicate that the Bunyans were at that period yeomen farmers who were going down in the world. However, they did not yet belong to the very poor. When Thomas Bunyan's father, who described himself as a "Pettie Chapman", died in 1641, he had some property to dispose of and had made a will.

Bunyan is the greatest representative of the common people to find a place in English literature. English social distinctions have never been rigid, and many small yeoman's sons in that age rose by grammar school and university to distinguish themselves in letters or the public service. But Bunyan's voice remains that of the popular culture of rural England, preserved much as it had been in the middle ages until it was swept away by the enclosures of the following century. He was loyal to his origins because he remained close to them. With the exception of preaching excursions to London in his later days, he spent his whole life in Bedford and its neighbourhood. The sixty years of his life bridge the Civil Wars, in which he played his minor part as conscript in a county levy, and the Puritan Revolution. His career as a sectarian preacher continued, in and out of prison, throughout the heroic age of Nonconformity under Charles II, and ended within a few days of the Revolution of 1688, which put an end to the religious struggle by incorporating the sects in the national life.

Thus Bunyan's life story is also a part of the militant phase of English Puritanism, and of its heroic resistance under persecution. *The Pilgrim's Progress* is one of the chief channels by which the Puritan spirit has entered the main stream of the English tradition. However, Bunyan did not live his whole life within the bounds of Nonconformist orthodoxy, and in this respect he is unlike other outstanding Puritan figures of the seventeenth century; both George Fox and Richard Baxter came of "godly" parents. He grew up as a typical member of a village community, not marked off from his fellows by any special pretensions to piety. The Puritanism of his life and his books retains much of this larger background: it owes most to the immensely diffused influence of the English Bible, and to the sturdy evangelical Christianity native to the eastern and east Midland counties. The extreme sectaries and fanatics came and went, but in the course of the seventeenth century this moderate Puritan ethos gradually permeated whole sections of the artisan and middle classes.

In Bunyan's age, the social and economic, as well as the religious life of the village, still revolved around the parish church. Conformity with its worship, signified by attendance at church on Sunday, was the essential badge, not merely of religious orthodoxy, but of participation in community life. Absence from church entailed a shilling fine levied under the warrant of a justice. If the absences continued, the offenders could be presented at the Archdeacon's court by the church-wardens. If, from one aspect, the state control of the church after the Elizabethan settlement might seem to secularize

PREFACE TO THE 1968 REISSUE

As well as making a few corrections in the text, I have taken the opportunity to revise and enlarge the bibliography.

Durham, 1967

PREFACE TO THE FIRST EDITION

THE following chapters are intended to furnish a general introduction to Bunyan's work which incorporates the findings of modern scholarship; I have tried to do equal justice to his individual spiritual history and to his place in the Puritan literary tradition.

In the forefront of my obligations comes a debt to the late Dr. F. E. Hutchinson, who criticized and encouraged my earliest work on Bunyan. My thanks are also due to Professor B. A. Wright and the Rev. Hubert Hoskins who read portions of the typescript and made valuable suggestions. The Editor of the *Review of English Studies* has kindly allowed me to make use of material originally published in that journal. Among many who have helped me with information or advice I must mention Mr. C. S. Lewis; Dr. G. F. Nuttall; Dr. E. A. Payne; Mr. Owen Watkins; and finally, Professor Basil Willey for his more than editorial helpfulness and patience.

Southampton, 1954

religion, it is possible on the other hand to see in its fusion of worship and civic obedience a continuation of the unified pattern of medieval life. Ralph Josselyn, Elizabethan parson and farmer, could write in his diary: "April 3rd.—Cow calved; administered the sacrament, only 14 present"—thus blending the sacred and the everyday with complete naturalness.

Bunyan's parents conformed to the Church of England, though his grandfather was once in trouble with the ecclesiastical court for abusing the churchwardens. The young John Bunyan grew up at the centre of this intense local life; he shared in its worship and played his part in its closely knit economy. It was a hard life, and from our standpoint a severely regimented one.[1] Wages were fixed by statute; the poor were sent to the House of Correction; sturdy beggars were beaten. The Archdeacon's court could still pry into the private lives of the parishioners as it had done in the days of Chaucer's Summoner. There were, however, compensations. To a certain extent even the humbler villagers could join in the management of their own affairs by holding offices like that of constable. Then, too, there were the relaxations suggested by the phrase "Merrie England"; into these the young Bunyan entered lustily. There were May games and dancing on the green in summer; violent forms of football and other sports after church on Sunday obstinately survived many post-Reformation attempts at suppression; and there was bell-ringing, which engaged both his skill and his keen musical sense.

All we know of his education is his own statement that "notwithstanding the meanness . . . of my Parents, it pleased God to put it into their Hearts to put me to School, to learn both to read and write"; he goes on to say that he soon forgot whatever he had learnt. If he did attend a grammar school, it may have been that at Houghton Conquest, which had a better reputation than the Bedford school at this period. Later, when he quoted Latin in *The Pilgrim's Progress*, he was to say boldly, "The Latin I borrow". Whether he had forgotten his "small Latin", or never learnt any, we do not know. No doubt he left school early to learn the trade of a brazier, or to work on the nine acres of land still belonging to the cottage at Bunyan's End; for elsewhere he says, "I never went to school to Aristotle or Plato, but was brought up at my father's house in a very mean condition, among a company of poor countrymen". It may have been the pride of yeoman stock with a name in the village that had sent him to school, and in such a household he would learn the characteristic yeoman virtues of thrift and independence and simplicity of manner. Many of that stock in the eastern counties inclined to Puritanism because their traditional sympathies were drawn to the austere living which it advocated.[2]

Looking back on this time when he was "without God in the world", Bunyan speaks of fearful dreams and visions which tormented him. Perhaps he was too anxious to search out in an ordinary childhood portents of the conversion that was yet to come. But there may have been early stirrings of the abnormal mental impulses he was later to suffer. In 1644 the sixteen-year-old boy received a shock which helped to precipitate his spiritual crises. His mother died in June, and his younger sister Margaret in July. In the following month his father married his third wife. Without indulging in baseless speculation about Bunyan's relations with his parents, we may conclude that the indecent haste of this marriage drove the boy's growing mind in upon itself. He was no Hamlet, but when his autobiography discovers him to us as he was a few years later, it is as a man who has withdrawn from the world of men to his inner life.

If he did feel alienated from his father and stepmother, he soon found an opportunity to cut himself off from the family. The war between King and Parliament had been in progress for two years. Bedfordshire was solidly for the Parliamentary interest. In November 1644 Bunyan was mustered in a Parliamentary levy and sent to the garrison at Newport Pagnell. The garrison commander was Sir Samuel Luke, the model for the hero of *Hudibras*. Bunyan was in the army until about July 1647, but he saw no active service. He tells the story of how, when he was drafted with others to besiege a certain place, the soldier who took his place was killed by a musket ball. Some of his biographers, relying upon an anonymous account of 1700, have suggested that he was present at the siege of

Leicester and its storming by Prince Rupert in 1645. There is however no evidence for this. Bunyan's name appears on a list of soldiers belonging to Colonel Charles O'Hara's regiment in June 1647, a body of men who had volunteered for service in Ireland. But the regiment never got to Ireland. It was disbanded in the following month, after a detachment of it had been marched as far as Chester. Perhaps this was Bunyan's furthest excursion from the Newport garrison.[3]

The real importance of his comparatively uneventful military life lay in the impressions made upon his youthful imagination by the militant Puritanism of the New Model Army. It was a complete change of atmosphere to move from the traditional, unintellectual Protestantism of Elstow to the preaching captains of the Ironsides whose religious convictions were consciously formulated according to a developed theological discipline. One of these soldiers turned preachers was the firebrand Paul Hobson who was arrested by Sir Samuel Luke for his heresies and sent to be examined before the authorities in London. Another was Henry Denne, a member of a London Baptist church, who was at this time on an evangelical tour of Bedfordshire and Cambridgeshire. We do not know whether there was any personal contact between him and Bunyan at this period, but fifteen years later when Bunyan himself had been re-baptized and become a preacher to conventicles, Denne took up his defence in print. The young George Fox, soon after he had left his family, and at the very beginning of his long years of wandering, "stayed awhile" in Newport Pagnell, remaining there till June 1644. Thus a gap of only a few months separated the sojourn in the same little town of the two most remarkable figures produced by English Puritanism.

Among all the sectarian preachers there was a strong feeling that their religion gave them a key to the great public events which were taking place. An opportunity was offered to establish the ideal Christian society, but first Antichrist had to be fought; these were, in Milton's phrase, "the wars of truth"; Cromwell's chaplain-general, William Dell, had said that the time was "the daies of the *Gospel*, wherein the *Mysterie* of *Iniquity* is become most mysterious".[4] The young conscript, as he listened to the Biblical rhetoric of the preaching captains, may have felt like the young Wordsworth in another revolutionary age:

> Bliss was it in that dawn to be alive,
> But to be young was very heaven.

It was, in fact, the crisis of the Puritan movement. It had already run through a whole century of development before Bunyan was swept up in its course.

II

In our own time we occasionally hear from journalists about "a return to belief", but never about a return to Puritanism. Puritanism appears as a closed account; and the ideals and habits of its seventeenth-century adherents may seem rather more remote than those of the Greeks of the fifth century B.C. But the influence of those ideals on every subsequent generation of Englishmen has been profound; it extends far beyond the membership of the Nonconformist churches, the nominal successors of the Puritan sects. In fact the Puritan element has become so thoroughly assimilated into our culture that we are apt to be a little shy and defensive about it, as if it were some not entirely respectable habit we were unable to eradicate. To take three or four quite different illustrations; the moral viewpoint displayed in George Eliot's novels cannot be fully appreciated without an understanding of this Puritan element in English life; nor can the peculiar atmosphere of English socialism, or Shelley's strange rage for perfection, or D. H. Lawrence's distrust of genteel society.

Puritanism is a way of life rather than a rigid system of ideas. There is implicit in Christianity the possibility of pressing the call to become holy and forsake the world to a logical extreme which flesh can hardly bear. When the demands made upon human nature actually are too great, a complete separation takes place between the worlds of the flesh and the spirit, and some form of Manicheism is the result; the central doctrine of the Incarnation is abused. But the Puritan stops short of heresy; he sees with a shock of horror which his English representatives call "conviction of sin" the infinite transcendence of God and the despicableness of man and his behaviour;

but he sees also, in the Bible as the Word of God, a strategic programme by which man's fallen estate may be redeemed. To achieve this programme he would turn human life into an armed camp: the Christian is seen as a soldier for ever moving through enemy country. All merely human institutions are involved in the disgrace of human nature. Consequently all historical manifestations of the Puritan spirit have involved either the regimentation of the state by the church in the interests of a purified Christianity, or the separation from society of small groups of believers who aim at the foundation of a holy community apart from the fabric of the state. This "church-type" and "sect-type" within Puritanism, as they have been called by the sociologist Troeltsch,[5] are represented respectively by the Calvinists who wished to impose a new and strict form of ecclesiastical organization on the whole community, and the various sects which broke away from Calvinism. Both were united in believing that religious experience was a direct personal relationship between God and the individual. But there were many conflicts in practice between this individualistic spirit and the Calvinist desire for an almost military discipline.

If the Puritan spirit is defined in this large and general sense, its work can be traced long before the Reformation. The separatist lay preachers are anticipated by the Lollards of the late fourteenth and early fifteenth centuries who were particularly active in the east Midlands. William Smith, prosecuted for heresy at Leicester in 1389, was an artisan, perhaps the first of many "mechanic preachers" to appear in Bunyan's own part of the country.[6] Chaucer's portrait of the poor Parson anticipates those Puritan pastors of the period before the Civil War who abstained from agitation and continued their work of preaching and saving souls within the church. Like them, his austere simplicity and sense of duty provide their own criticism of the pluralists and place-seekers:

> He waited after no pompe and reverence,
> Ne maked him a spiced conscience,
> But Christes loore and his apostles twelve
> He taughte, but first he folwed it hymselve.

The later Puritan ministers, too, devoted their energies to teaching the essentials of Christianity. Also, the popular preaching of the later middle ages, especially that of the mendicant orders, established habits of exposition and illustration which survived in the pulpit in Tudor and Stuart times.

But the term Puritan originated in a more specialized sense.[7] It first came to be used about 1563 as a term of reproach for the party within the Church of England which felt that Elizabeth's settlement had not gone far enough in the direction of reformation. These men were followers of Calvin; some of them had been in exile in Geneva, the Calvinist stronghold, during Mary's reign. Though they first came into conflict with the authorities over questions of ecclesiastical discipline, it was the theology of Calvin which provided the dynamic principle behind the whole movement. Calvin gave a logical, sixteenth-century form to "the agonised conscience"[8] of the temperamental Puritanism which recurs from age to age, since St. Paul said in *The Epistle to the Romans*, "The evil I would not do, I do". The terrifying doctrine of predestination follows naturally from the acceptance of the gulf between man's absolute depravity and the infinite goodness of God. According to this doctrine, God has before the beginning of time predestined certain men to be saved and others to be damned. Man achieves salvation through no merits of his own, but only through the free grace of Christ given in election.

The problem for the Calvinist, then, is how to ascertain whether he is among the number of the elect. Since good works are of no account, and any total reliance on sacramental means of grace is dismissed as idolatry, the believer must search his heart and minutely examine his daily conduct for evidence of his election. For although he cannot earn merit by acting well, his moral excellence may be a token of saving faith. Thus Calvin's determinism did not have the demoralizing effect on conduct which might have been expected. Only a few fanatics, called in Bunyan's day the Antinomians, believed that ordinary morality was superseded by the new law, and the elect could do as they pleased. The mass of Puritans led a life of disciplined moral effort directed towards the discovery of some assurance of their salvation. It is important to notice that the discipline was an intellectual discipline. Conversion was not a sudden unheaval, such as took place under some emotional perversions of Calvinism in later periods. It might be spread over a number of years, and it was supposed to result in the sanctification of all the mental and practical activities of the convert. As the Elizabethan Puritan John Dod said: "The godly do good works to confirm their faith, and to assure and certify their consciousness of election". There was always the appeal from theological dogma to the religious experience of the individual.

The controversy between the Puritans and Elizabeth's archbishops was fought out over questions of ritual and church government. The Calvinists advocated Presbyterianism on the Genevan model: the people were to choose their own ministers and the ministers were to elect a central assembly of presbyters. Bishops seemed to them unbiblical and unapostolic. They also disapproved of some of the forms and ceremonies retained in Elizabeth's compromise between the new and the old religion; vestments, confirmation, and the use of the sign of the cross, appeared to them to savour of Catholicism. There was little argument about theology, because the main Reformed doctrines, especially Calvin's statement of them, had become very widely diffused among English people. The ordinary London citizen, if he was not a Puritan and went to the theatre, could enjoy the fun at the expense of the "Precisians", with their dark clothes, sing-song voices, and pious sayings (like Ben Jonson's Zeal-of-the-Land Busy in *Bartholomew Fair*). But like them he believed that he was justified by faith and not by his own good deeds, and that human nature was utterly corrupt. The doctrine of predestination found its way into the Thirty-Nine Articles (Article XVII).

A more important bond still between the Puritan and the ordinary man of the age was their common assumption that the worship of God was the primary duty of man's life, an assumption as much medieval as Calvinist. The difference between the Puritan and his contemporaries can be seen in his attitude to the Bible. While all believed it to be the inspired Word of God, the exponents of the Anglican *via media* were prepared to accept some guidance from other sources for the

B

conduct of church and state: the Anglican apologist Hooker could give a place to tradition, and to the law of nature which was imprinted in the hearts of men. The Puritan was not prepared to do this. The rationalist approach of Calvinism to theology and Biblical interpretation caused a considerable relaxation of fundamentalism in the generations after Calvin. But for the educated Puritan the Bible remained the key to all knowledge, human and divine. From it he drew his principles of politics and church government and his standards of literary criticism. Even the humanist Milton could feel compelled on this score to disparage the classics; for what were elegance and human wisdom when set beside truth itself?

> Remove their swelling Epithetes thick laid
> As varnish on a Harlots cheek, the rest,
> Thin sown with aught of profit or delight,
> Will far be found unworthy to compare
> With *Sion's* songs, to all true tasts excelling,
> Where God is prais'd aright, and Godlike men,
> The Holiest of Holies, and his Saints. [9]

In Elizabeth's reign the Puritan party first emerged as a political force under Thomas Cartwright, Lady Margaret Professor of Divinity at Cambridge, who had been educated in Geneva. Cambridge was a Puritan centre, and Emmanuel and Sidney Sussex colleges, founded late in the sixteenth century, were important Puritan foundations. Elizabeth was firm but tactful in her dealings with the reform party. But at the Hampton Court Conference in 1604 James I made it bluntly plain to the dissident ministers that for him "No bishop" meant "No king", and that they would achieve none of their demands by peaceable agreement. From then on the final conflict was inevitable, and was only hastened by the high church ascendancy of Laud. The Puritans, whose ideal aim was to make use of the state so as to confirm their own authority over men's souls and conduct, found themselves driven by the logic of events to fight for freedom from state interference and to attempt to wrest concessions from the civil power.

III

The political efforts of Cartwright and his successors were abortive. Since they were unable to win their way on a national scale, the Puritans had to direct their spiritual energy into other channels. The most important development during the whole century from the return of the Genevan exiles to the Civil War was the gradual growth of a school of preachers and pastors, who, like Chaucer's poor Parson, attended to the needs of the individual soul and left the struggles of the time to take care of themselves.

These men were the natural successors of the late medieval popular preachers of the mendicant orders; their Calvinism gave a new life to the more austere kind of medieval piety. Cambridge was their nursery, and their influence was strongest about London and in the eastern counties. It worked in two ways: through preaching, and through the intimate direction of souls. Preaching the Word was second only in importance to the Word itself. The demand for preachers in many parishes in Tudor and Stuart times always exceeded the supply, since only a limited number of the clergy were licensed to preach by a government jealous of their political influence; in those days a sermon had the propaganda value of a newspaper. Richard Baxter describes the conditions in Shropshire, in his boyhood early in the seventeenth century:

> We lived in a Country that had but little Preaching at all. In the village where I was born there was four Readers successively in Six years time, ignorant Men, and two of them immoral in their lives. . . . In the Village where my Father lived, there was a Reader of about Eighty years of Age that never preached, and had two Churches about Twenty miles distant: his Eyesight failing him, he said Common Prayer without Book; but for the Reading of the Psalms and Chapters he got a Common Thresher and Day-Labourer one year, and a Taylor another year . . . only three or four constant competent Preachers lived near us, and those (though Conformable all save one) were the common Marks of the People's Obloquy and Reproach, and any that had but gone to hear them, when he had no Preaching at home, was made the Derision of the Vulgar Rabble, under the odious name of a *Puritane.*[10]

Thus the name Puritan came to be applied to many earnest "spiritual" preachers, whether or not they agitated against ceremonies and the prayer-book. In the same way, as soon as Chaucer's Parson had begun simply and seriously to expound the Gospel, the ruffianly Shipman called out "Ho, I smell a Lollard in the wind!"

The preachers were also spiritual directors. Protestantism had abolished the confessional but the preoccupation with the inward evidence for salvation created a host of introspective problems demanding the advice of an expert. The advice was given in conferences of ministers, when questions concerning conversion were propounded and answered, or sometimes in private exhortation. It was said of the great Cambridge Puritan William Perkins that he was "An excellent Chirurgeon at joynting of a broken soul, and at stating of a doubtful conscience".[11] Sermons, too, were brought home to the problems of the individual, concentrating on the "uses" or practical applications of doctrine. The preachers turned from technical theology to a descriptive psychology of the process of conversion; it was all very English and empirical. The different landmarks of the spiritual life were mapped out: first, conviction of sin; then vocation or calling, when the Christian had evidence of his election and separation from the world; then, justification, the achievement of a saving faith; then, sanctification, the growth in holiness of life; and finally glorification, the end of the pilgrim's progress.

The influence of this pastoral work was incalculable. It meant that the essentially learned character of early Elizabethan Puritanism was transformed into a popular movement. Large sections of the new middle class in the towns and of the independent yeomen and small farmers in the Midlands and the west became inbued with the Puritan ethos. A certain type of piety grew up admirably adapted to the life of the middle groups in English society: it was earnest, energetic and self-restrained, and always directed beyond present instruments to an ulterior goal. Its exponents were assiduous in private and family prayers; they were constant in self-examination and often communicated the results to a diary. Obviously the sins most incident to such idealism were to be found at the opposite poles of hypocrisy and self-righteousness, but there were many who sustained the rigours of their self-imposed discipline. The word Puritan lost its derogatory sense and came to denote the practitioners of this way of life, as well as the representatives of a Presbyterian point of view in church matters.

This is illustrated by a pamphlet published in the period of Bunyan's military service, John Geree's *The Character of an Old English Puritane, or Non-Conformist* (1646).[12] Looking back from the storm and stress of the Civil War which had broken the unity of Puritanism, dividing Presbyterian against Independent, and both against the sectaries of the left wing, the writer is able to create an idyllic picture of a godly person of the old school. The political aspect is at a discount: the non-conformity of his nonconformist hardly enters into the portrait:

> He reverenced Authority keeping within its sphaere: but durst not under pretence of subjection to the high powers, worship God after the traditions of men.

He prefers prayers "varied according to present wants and and occasions", but does not consider set forms unlawful, like the extremists who, according to the Anglican South, would talk out the prayers at the church door and only take their seats for the sermon.[13] But the sermon of course is what he values most.

> He esteemed that preaching best wherein was most of God, least of man, when vaine flourishes of wit, and words were declined, and the demonstration of Gods Spirit and power studied. . . . He accounted perspicuity the best grace of a Preacher: And that method best, which was most helpfull to understanding, affection and memory.

Bunyan, too, could say: "I preached what I felt, what I smartingly did feel". The Puritan advocated and practised the plain style, in contrast to the humanistic or metaphysical elegance of some high Anglican preachers; he took the simplicity of the Gospel as his model and aimed to reach the hearts

of simple men. Finally, Geree's example is a strict observer of
the Sabbath and "His family he endeavoured to make a Church".
A nation within a nation was growing up, and many absorbed
the Puritan message in their own homes, before they sat under
godly pulpits; Baxter's early years were like this:

> It pleased God to instruct and change my Father, by the bare
> reading of the Scriptures in private, without either Preaching,
> or Godly Company, or any other Books but the Bible: And God
> made him the Instrument of my first Convictions, and Approba-
> tion of a Holy Life, as well as of my Restraint from the grosser
> sort of Lives.

Everywhere sounds the note of disciplined effort towards
the achievement of the holy community, whether on a household or on a national scale; Geree employs the military image
to be met with so often in Puritan literature:

> His whole life hee accounted a warfare, wherein Christ was his
> Captaine, his armes, prayers and teares. The Crosse his Banner,
> and his word *vincit qui patitur*.

Bunyan was to describe that Christian warfare more fully
in his second great allegory. He had access to the vast literature
of popular guides to godliness which had been produced in the
eighty years before the Civil War. His debt to the preachers
and writers of this moderate, non-political Puritanism was
shared with other members of the artisan class whom the
Puritan Revolution stirred into thinking for themselves about
religion. Perkins, John Dod, Richard Greenham, Richard
Sibbes, and others, had persuaded their audiences that nothing
was more important than saving their own souls, and that
only they themselves were able to do so; a corollary of this
not foreseen by the preachers was that those thus convinced
of their own spiritual freedom would allow no human authority
to stand in their way, not even that of ordained ministers
from Cambridge. Religious individualists, often laymen,
formed their own independent congregations in order to
worship according to their own lights. William Smith the
Lollard had his spiritual descendants, as well as Chaucer's

Parson, and Bunyan was one of them. Though he came to absorb much from the general tradition of evangelical Puritanism, it was the sectaries, the wild men of the movement, who first seized his attention.

The sectarian impulse latent in Calvinism had first made itself felt during the political frustration of Puritanism under Elizabeth. Robert Browne was the first Independent or Congregationalist: he promulgated his "Reformation without tarrying for anie" at Norwich in 1580–81. An offshoot of these early Independents or Brownists, having met with persecution, fled to Holland and founded the English church at Amsterdam. The separatist conception of a church was a close voluntary association of believers. It was carried a step further by those who advocated adult believers' baptism. In their own age they were commonly known as Anabaptists but were later called Baptists. There had been Anabaptists in the Reformation period in Germany, and their revolutionary rule in Munster left unhappy memories of bloodshed and fanaticism. But the English Baptists owe little or nothing to Continental influence. They enter history in 1609 when John Smith separated himself from the Amsterdam congregation by baptizing himself. A Baptist church was founded at Leyden, and Smith's former associate Thomas Helwys returned to England to establish a community in London. It was members of the Leyden church who, joined by separatists from England, sailed in 1620 to the first settlements in Massachusetts Bay.

The gatherings of Baptists in London grew rapidly. Helwys and his successors were General Baptists, that is to say they believed in a general salvation and rejected the orthodox Calvinist doctrine of election. The Particular, or Calvinist Baptists, became organized a little later, in 1616, but their churches soon outnumbered those of the General Baptists. Both branches agreed in advocating the separation of church and state and complete liberty of conscience; they opposed tithes and a paid clergy. Henry Denne, who preached in Newport Pagnell during Bunyan's stay there, was a General Baptist, belonging to Lamb's church in Bell Alley.

The Baptists were the most numerous and vigorous of a number of sects which proliferated with extraordinary richness

and extravagance in the revolutionary period of 1640–60.
The sectaries were generally speaking drawn from lower social
strata than the orthodox Puritans and the more conservative
Independents. To approach their mode of thought and worship
is to enter a different world. The keynote of Puritanism had
been intellectual discipline, respectability and good order;
though the Puritan maintained the supremacy of Scripture,
he would never have dreamed it could be so interpreted as to
run counter to these comfortable principles. But the Cambridge
intellectuals had sown the wind to reap the whirlwind. The
behaviour of the sectaries at their meetings ranged from wild
enthusiasm to pathological eccentricity: they were carried away
to testify in the Spirit; they waged a bitter pamphlet warfare
against a University-trained clergy; and their pulpits were
filled by cobblers, buttonmakers, ostlers, and other "mechanics".
There were mass baptisms by immersion in rivers, celebrations
of the Jewish Sabbath, and revivals of the practice of anointing.
And further still to the left, on the extreme lunatic fringe,
were the Fifth-Monarchy Men, who believed that only King
Jesus could bring about a political settlement of the kingdom,
the Muggletonians whose leaders declared they were the
witnesses mentioned in the eleventh chapter of Revelation,
and the Ranters who were reported to indulge in fearful excesses.

The extremists were strong in Cromwell's army, and were
described by an indignant Presbyterian as

> strange monsters, having their heads of Enthusiasme, their
> bodies of Antinomianisme, their thighs of Familisme, their leggs
> and feet of Anabaptisme, their hands of Arminianisme and
> Libertinisme as the great vein going thorow the whole; in one
> word, the great Religion of that sort of men in the Army is
> liberty of conscience, and liberty of preaching.[14]

It was the army's resistance to Presbyterian tyranny, when it
found that "New Presbyter is but old Priest writ large",
which made this liberty possible. Common also to all the sectarian groups was a tendency to regard revelation as progressive.
Even more than other good Protestants they looked forward
to some great consummation yet to be. It was natural that
during the Civil Wars this aspiration should take a political and

social form, not only among Fifth Monarchy extremists; from Milton to the fanatic preachers, it was an age of watching and waiting for the final perfecting of Reformation which should result in the rule of the saints. Men were ready, in the words supposed to have been addressed by John Robinson to the party leaving Leyden for the new world, "to receive whatever Truth shall be made known to them from the written Word of God".[15] Lucy Hutchinson, the wife of a Baptist army officer, rejoiced in the advantageous time of her birth:

> It was not in the midnight of popery, nor in the dawn of the gospel's restored day, when light and shades were blended, but when the Sun of truth was exalted in his progress, and hastening towards a meridian glory.

It was at this time of expectation and desire, when the drums were beating and the pamphlets streaming from the presses, that the young Bunyan had his first impressions of the world beyond the horizon of Elstow. When he was demobilized in the summer of 1647 the elected representatives of the army were debating the destinies of the kingdom at Putney. Sectarian junior officers had come to the forefront of affairs, and some of them, the Levellers, were demanding political as well as religious equality for all men.

IV

Returned to Elstow and civilian life, Bunyan assimilated the new ideas in his own time. His own account of his life, *Grace Abounding*, written twenty years later during his imprisonment, is sparse in external facts; it is a spiritual autobiography, and the external facts of any moment were but few. He followed his father's trade of tinkering, and a few years after his demobilization he married. There is no record of the marriage, and the fact that the wife used to tell her husband about the godly life of her father suggests that she may have come from outside the Bedford area. The couple were poor, "not having so much household stuff as a Dish or

Spoon", but she brought him two religious books, Arthur Dent's *The Plaine Mans Path-way to Heaven* and Bishop Lewis Bayly's *The Practice of Piety*. Arthur Dent was a Puritan clergyman in Essex, and his book was one of the most widely read of the popular devotional guides which abounded before the Civil War. Between 1601 when it first appeared and 1640 the work ran through twenty-five editions, and by the fortieth edition in 1704 it has been estimated that over a hundred thousand copies had been printed. Its nervous, colloquial style, spiced with shrewd aphorisms, recalls the tradition of the medieval vernacular homily. Bunyan learnt much from it concerning the technique of didactic fiction. He also remembered particular things in the book: his Man with the Muck Rake in Part Two of *The Pilgrim's Progress* recalls a vivid phrase of Dent about "the gripple mucke-rakers who had as leeve part with their blood, as their goods".[16] *The Practice of Piety* is less interesting, since it is not a fiction but a devotional manual; though its author was destined for a bishopric, it starts on an uncompromisingly Calvinistic note: "Wee will therefore lay down the knowledge of Gods Majesty and Mans Misery, as the first and chiefest grounds of the Practice of Piety". Bunyan's unknown father-in-law was certainly a Puritan of the old-fashioned type; "he would reprove and correct Vice, both in his House, and amongst his Neighbours". The absence of any reference to Bunyan's father suggests that he may have been a very different man.

Under the influence of his wife Bunyan, who had apparently been a wild young man, began to make some outward profession of respectability. There is no evidence that he was really dissolute, but looking back from the high standards of his autobiography, he seemed to himself a person of "prodigious Profaneness". He was a great swearer, and he took pleasure in bell-ringing. The horror he felt for the former offence may seem to us disproportionate, and his shame over the latter entirely misapplied; but Bunyan's feelings were those of an age for which the smallest detail of outward behaviour was the sign of an inward and spiritual state. To the Puritan bell-ringing was a frivolous superfluity, no necessary part of worship; pastimes profaned the Sabbath, and even the mildest oath was

a kind of atheism. There were laws against swearing which the
Commonwealth tried to enforce; a justice of the peace described it as "the Common Sin of our Age".[17]

Bunyan's sensibility was still child-like: it was deeply
rooted in the material components of his life, though he was now
beginning to undergo the torment of a desire for something
not to be reached through the daily round of hard work and
rough play. At this time he could vex himself with naïve
questionings as to whether he belonged to the Israelites or not,
and a little later he nearly commanded the puddles on the road
between Elstow and Bedford to dry up, as a test of his faith.
He had not yet sorted out in his mind the new ideas he had
absorbed about grace and sanctification. He felt dimly that
they must apply to his condition, but his own attempt to make
them fit his case only increased his brooding anxiety; and
always he brought the test of faith down to deeds and things.

At this period he began to attend both morning and
evening prayer at Elstow Church, superstitiously admiring
"the High place, Priest, Clerk, Vestment, Service"; this
high place can only have been a table and the vestment a
plain Geneva gown; the vicar, Christopher Hall, retained his
living throughout the interregnum, and must therefore have
satisfied the requirements of the Parliamentary commissioners,
though he cannot have been active in suppressing Sunday
sports in which Bunyan continued to indulge.

Years of darkness and spiritual despair were now drawing
upon him. Probably the crisis had been forming within him
since early years. History had decided that it should be cast
into the mould of a classic Puritan conversion. But his extraordinary nervous vitality gave a peculiar dramatic emphasis
to every stage of spiritual growth. Mere terror of sin came first,
the fear of the Mosaic law which was entirely in accordance with
the handbooks. But obviously for Bunyan the experience was
a naked and independent one; there was a real, though shapeless
terror, which later lent itself easily to rationalization in Calvinist
terms. As he played one day at a Sunday game he seemed to
hear a voice from heaven saying "Wilt thou leave thy sins and go
to Heaven, or have thy sins and go to Hell?" Slowly and pain-
fully he gave up the old man; first his swearing, then his

bell-ringing (though he lingered to watch the ringers, till fears that a judgement would cause the main beam to fall on him drove him from the tower); finally, a year later, his dancing. None of this was trivial; it answered to the need to make all things anew in his life. He began to live what the Puritans called a legal life: he tried to live by the commandments. ("I was all this while ignorant of Jesus Christ, and going about to establish my own Righteousness.") Of course his despair became greater. Then one day he came upon three or four poor women sitting in the sun and talking about a new birth and the work of God in their hearts. This was his introduction to the Bedford separatist church and the decisive step in his history.

NOTES

CHAPTER I

1. There is a discussion of the community life of the village in Eleanor Trotter, *Seventeenth Century Life in the Country Parish* (Cambridge, 1919), pp. 178–98.

2. For the growth of Puritanism among the yeomen, see Mildred Campbell, *The English Yeoman* (New Haven, 1943), pp. 292–3.

3. The evidence for Bunyan's military service is described in John Brown, *John Bunyan: his Life, Times, and Work*, revised edition by F. M. Harrison (1928), pp. 46–50.

4. William Dell, *The Tryal of Spirits Both in Teachers & Hearers* (1660), p. 5.

5. Ernst Troeltsch, *The Social Teaching of the Christian Churches* (English trans. by Olive Wyon, 1931), II, pp. 590, 679–80.

6. R. B. McFarlane, *John Wycliffe and the Beginnings of English Nonconformity* (1952), pp. 139–41.

7. On the earlier history of Puritanism, especially its intellectual development, see the invaluable study by William Haller, *The Rise of Puritanism* (Columbia, 1938).

8. George Santayana, *Winds of Doctrine* (1940), p. 189: "Calvinism . . . is an expression of the agonised conscience".

9. Milton, *Paradise Regain'd*, IV, 343–9.

10. Richard Baxter, *Reliquiae Baxterianae* (1696), I, pp. 1–2.

11. Thomas Fuller, *The Holy State* (1642), p. 90.

12. Reprinted in *Church Quarterly Review*, Vol. CLXVIII (1949), pp. 65–71.

13. Robert South, *Twelve Sermons upon Several Subjects and Occasions* (1697–8), III, p. 204.

14. Thomas Edwards, *Gangraena* (3rd. ed. 1646), p. 14.

15. Daniel Neal, *A History of the Puritans*, II (1732), p. 129.

16. *The Plaine Mans Path-way to Heaven* (ed. 1617), p. 91.

17. A. H. A. Hamilton, *Quarter Sessions from Queen Elizabeth to Queen Anne* (1878), p. 190.

THE LIFE OF A SECTARY

I

IT was in the period 1651–3 that Bunyan first came in contact with the Bedford congregation, which was then in its infancy. Its character was broad and generous and free from dogmatism about the externals of worship. The statement of first principles in the *Church Book* suggests an idealized expression of the Puritanism of the sect-type.[1] Long before the Commonwealth period there had been persons in Bedford who "had in some measure separated themselves from the prelaticall superstition; and had agreed to search after the non-conformity men, such as in those dayes did beare the name of Puritanes". The fortunes of this little group could be paralleled in many places up and down England. Without having any set form of organization, they met to edify one another; the wealthier members helped the poorer and kept open house for godly ministers. Among them were some men of substance. Two of their founding fathers, John Grew and John Eston, had been mayors of Bedford, and the latter was a justice of the peace. When the Long Parliament brought freedom from episcopacy, they inclined more to Independency than to Presbyterianism, and chose their own pastor. They dealt with problems of doctrine and discipline as they arose, thus producing their own simple pattern of the course of Christian ecclesiastical development. The first pastor, John Gifford, was a remarkable man. He had been a Royalist major and escaped from prison where he was awaiting execution for his part in the Kentish rising of 1648. He took shelter in Bedford and practised medicine, and then, after living for some time the life of a gamester and debauchee, underwent a Puritan conversion; he soon revealed to the local saints his gift as a lay preacher. At his instigation, and after

much seeking God in prayer, they formed themselves into a
church in 1650 and made him their minister.

> Now the principle upon which they thus entered into fellowship
> one with another, and upon which they did afterwards receive those
> that were added to their body, and fellowship, was ffaith in Christ,
> and Holines of life, without respect to this or that circumstance,
> or opinion in outward, and circumstantiall things.

John Gifford left a personal testament to the church in which he
cautioned them against divisions over externals:

> Concerning separation from the Church about Baptisme, laying on
> of hands, Anoynting with Oyls, Psalmes, or any externalls; I
> charge every one of you respectively, that none of you be found
> guilty of this great evill.

Gifford and his successor John Burton were moderate
Baptists, who although they administered believer's baptism
to those who desired it, did not make it a condition of communion with the church. Bunyan meeting, as the church came
to be called, remained loyal to this liberal tradition, and together
with a few other congregational groups organized on similar
principles, formed the open-communion wing of the Particular
Baptists, as opposed to the Strict Particulars who denounced
paedobaptism and insisted on the immersion of their adult
converts.

There was a democratic spirit at work in Bedford as in
some other Baptist congregations. Gifford reminded his flock
that in Christ there was neither bond nor free, and warned
them against the bad example of offering seats to wealthy
members in time of prayer. Although the Baptists were bitterly
opposed to the Quakers, there are resemblances to early
Quakerism in the early history of the Bedford church: women
played an important part, those members who had "most of the
demonstration of the Spirit, and of power" could address
the meeting, and there was a similar stress on outward simplicity;
Eston and Grew paid fines in March 1651 for appearing in the
council chamber without their aldermen's gowns.[2] General
Baptist influence was also present in the area, reinforced by

the recent preaching tours of Henry Denne and William Erbury; this made for tenderness towards the individual conscience, and also for a certain degree of political and social radicalism.

There is a mysterious passage in Gifford's death-bed letter:

> Let the promises made to be accomplished in the latter dayes, be often urged before the Lord in your comings together, and forget not your brethren in bonds.

There was no strictly religious persecution under the Protectorate, but the reference is probably to the imprisonment of Fifth Monarchy agitators, who had hoped that Cromwell would bring about the rule of the Saints. Two of these, Feake and Rogers, were still in custody when Gifford died on 21st September, 1655. The promises would be those of Daniel and Revelation about the overthrow of the Beast, and the prisoners had identified the Beast with the Protector. The *Church Book* does not give the impression of a community of fanatics, but millenarian ideas were very widely diffused among the Baptists; there was the small group of wilder enthusiasts who believed in some precise system of dating for the events prophesied in Revelation and were ready to engage in treasonable plots to back their identifications of the Beast, the Two Witnesses, Gog and Magog; but there were also numbers of more sober Puritans in the army and the gathered churches who believed without indulgence in cryptograms or arithmetical speculation, that these were the days of the Gospel, that Cromwell had had the opportunity of establishing some kind of theocracy at the time of Barebone's Parliament in 1653, and that by dismissing that assembly and assuming personal power he had disobeyed a heaven-sent mandate. In 1657 the rumour that Cromwell was about to accept the crown occasioned a wave of disapproval among the sectaries, and members of the Bedford congregation sent a petition to Whitehall on the subject.[3]

Little is know of Bunyan's relations with Gifford. He met him early in his spiritual crisis, when oppressed by his sense of his own unworthiness and still little schooled in Calvinist dialectic; Gifford may have recognized a fellow-spirit in Bunyan, another strong and passionate nature which had to undergo division before it could be reconciled with itself. He thought well of the young tinker from the start ("from little grounds", Bunyan adds), and invited him to his house to hear others giving an account of their spiritual experience. He became a member of the church in 1653, but the worst of his inner struggles were still before him. He was beset by temptations to utter despair. Voices seemed to whisper to him that the time of grace was past and that he had no hope of salvation. His new friends would tell him that the solution to his anxieties was to be found in the Bible; he began to look into it "with new eyes", and to study carefully the Pauline epistles, repositories of the theology of grace and election. Verse by verse he searched for a text which would resolve his doubts and either lead him out on the further side of despair or convince him that he was totally abandoned. To look for personal messages in Scripture was a sectarian habit, but he gave it his own peculiar naïve intensity; he would spend a whole year in tracking down a phrase of comfort which had imprinted itself upon his mind, and then be dismayed at finding it in the apocryphal books. His soul became a battleground in which conflicting texts jostled for mastery. In *Grace Abounding* he calls his temptations "storms", and they buffeted him with almost physical violence. The voices within urged him not merely to despair but to make his destruction certain by some act of blasphemy which would amount to betraying Christ. The words, "Sell him, sell him, sell him", seemed to be repeated hundreds of times on end, and at last as he lay in bed one morning, worn out with struggling against his obsessions, the thought came to him, "Let him go, if he will". He had now reached the blackest part of his misery, and from this point onwards his condition became lightened. The total surrender brought a kind of release: the spring of self-torture had snapped and there were no dark places left in his consciousness which he had not now fully explored. The beautiful image by which he described his collapse suggests this release of tension: "down fell I, as a Bird that is shot from the top of a tree".

Gradually, among the scraps of scripture that hurried

through his mind, curses gave way to promises of election. "This returned upon me, as an echo or sounding-again, *I have loved thee with an everlasting love.*" The spiritual serenity which now followed the storm was consonant with the highly dramatic psychology of grace Bunyan was learning from Gifford: it was most fitting that he who had found himself utterly unworthy should receive a gift of grace which was utterly free; in his own language:

> I never saw those heights and depths in Grace, and Love, and Mercy, as I saw after this temptation. Great Sins do draw out great Grace.

The process of religious conversion in an individual must always remain mysterious, whatever the psychological terms in which its outward progress may be interpreted. But it is also surprising, at a more mundane level, that his health and sanity survived the stresses he endured. His whole being was given up to the religious experience; as in Kierkegaard's leap into faith, or Pascal's wager, he ventured all or nothing. Other uneducated men who became sectaries often proclaimed their new allegiance by a flamboyant display of Scripture language; they discoursed of tabernacles and fiery flying rolls, of "laying hold on" or "getting into" Christ, and were inclined to forget their unregenerate past entirely in the exotic novelty of such a style. But Bunyan is temperate in his use of this jargon, and his most telling phrases reflect the regular beauty of common life which remains a constant backcloth to his internal drama:

> I should in these days, often in my greatest Agonies, ever flounce towards the Promise (as the Horses do towards sound Ground that yet stick in the Mire).

His is an experience at too deep a level to be in need of exotic imagery to express it. He gives the impression that extraordinary things are happening to an ordinary man, not to a person psychologically abnormal; he resents his divorce from familiar life. For in spite of his contact with the Bedford congregation,

C

little is said about it in his account of the crisis; it is a lonely
struggle:

> I lifted up my head, but methought I saw as if the Sun that
> shineth in the Heavens did grudge to give light, and as if the
> very stones in the Street, and tiles upon the Houses, did bend
> themselves against me; methought that they all combined together
> to banish me out of the world. . . . O how happy, now, was every
> creature over I was. For they stood fast and kept their station,
> but I was gone and lost.

He dreams that he sees the holy women of Bedford in the
sun on the other side of a mountain and that he is pushing and
striving to reach them. The Calvinist ascesis meant the isolation
of the convert, and Bunyan's personal terror since childhood
seems to have been a fear of being cut off from the ordinary
world of men. A peculiar feature of his experience is the
blending of the slow, chequered progress usual in the classic
Puritan case-histories with a vehement emotionalism in his
moments of justification which is Lutheran rather than Calvinist.
Thus the words "Thou art my Love, thou art my Love, and
nothing shall separate thee from my Love", sound over and
over again in his mind, and sudden surges of feeling are expressed
by frequent ejaculations ("Oh! how was my soul led from truth
to truth by God", "Oh! now I know, I know"); on the other
hand, his more morbid temptations are mixed with simple
intellectual doubts:

> Every one doth think his own religion rightest, both Jews and
> Moors and Pagans! and how if all our Faith, and Christ, and
> Scriptures, should be but a Think so too?

and when he has overcome his irrational impulses to despair,
he is able to analyse them as partly the work of Satan, partly
the result of his own intellectual confusion. On the whole
the emotional element predominates, but there is a firm
theological framework; God remains apart from man, and
Bunyan detests any loose religious subjectivism; he hears
voices, whether of temptation or of consolation, but he will
not acknowledge an inner light. He had, indeed, read a tattered
translation of Luther's *Commentary on Galatians*, and this

may have contributed to his emotional attitude to justification, but the more dryly intellectualist approach of academic Puritanism was foreign to his nature; for him religion was a matter of mastery over the will and imagination. The blend of Calvinist orthodoxy and sectarian religious feeling is a happy one: he escapes theological dryness, while keeping his feet on the ground and avoiding the excesses of the Ranters and Quakers.

Soon his last scruples were removed and he entered fully into the life of the little meeting. According to its rule he had to give an account of his spiritual experience before being admitted to communion; *Grace Abounding* no doubt grew out of his testimony. The length and formidable character of the temptations, as well as the convert's eloquence, contributed to raise his prestige. Meanwhile, in 1653, Gifford had been presented by the Bedford Corporation to the living of St. John's, which was in their gift. The Bedford separatists, like others, became a part of the Cromwellian establishment, and for the first and last time Baptists found themselves belonging to a state church. Lay preachers still enjoyed freedom and they now had access to beneficed pulpits. Gifford died in 1655, and after a dispute over the presentation which was settled by Cromwell, he was succeeded in the following January by John Burton, a young man in weak health who lived only a few years. Bunyan had already delivered private discourses among the brethren; in 1656 he began to preach in public. His gift of natural vigour and conviction soon discovered itself; until *The Pilgrim's Progress* was published he was better known among his fellow-sectaries as a preacher than as a writer.

He was an active church member in other ways, visiting lapsed brethren and likely converts to examine their state of mind, as was the custom of the community. There was much travelling up and down, for some of the brethren lived in villages outside Bedford, like Gamlingay and Westoning, and ample opportunity for the future writer to study human types. He was already a father and like his own Christian had his family about him in the years of his spiritual crisis. A blind daughter, Mary, had been born in 1650, and another daughter, Elizabeth,

in 1654. Both were baptized at Elstow, which indicates a
conservatism that could nevertheless find its place within the
comprehensiveness of Gifford's church. In 1655 he moved from
Elstow to Bedford, where he would be at the centre of the
community.

II

In 1656 Bunyan published his first book, a pamphlet against
the Quakers called *Some Gospel Truths Opened*. The Friends
had spread rapidly in Bedfordshire after the arrival of their
first evangelist, William Dewsbury, in 1654. John Crook, a
county magistrate, had been convinced and turned his house at
Beckrings Park into a centre of entertainment for the movement. Baptists had good cause to be alarmed at its progress,
for the Quakers were their rivals for the allegiance of the
common people; George Fox had gained his first following
among a group of "shattered Baptists", and both sects had
many ideas in common; both were democratic, anti-clerical, and
believed in any man's freedom to testify in the spirit. Burton and
Bunyan felt that the special characteristics of their message
were being exploited by their rivals. Public disputations took
place between May and November 1656 at the Market Cross
in Bedford, and elsewhere. The young Edward Burrough
was the Quaker protagonist, and his addresses were the occasion
of Bunyan's tract.[4] Availing himself of the robust controversial
manners of the time, Bunyan called Burrough "a grossly
railing Rabshakeh". Apart from professional rivalry, he was
genuinely terrified at the early Quaker doctrine of the inner
light and at their treatment of Scripture. His literal, objective
type of mind laid supreme stress on the Bible as a precise
historical narrative so that Quaker emphasis on an inner Christ
seemed to him a blasphemous neglect of Scripture; and his
smarting sense of sin made him intolerant of the apparent
complacency of those who claimed to possess Christ in their
hearts. Burrough replied to Bunyan, who answered him in a
second book, *A Vindication of Some Gospel Truths Opened*
(1657). In spite of its unfortunate acrimoniousness, and the
pettiness of many of the points either side scored against the

other, the controversy is an important demonstration of Bunyan's passionate belief in the objective character of revelation, his distrust of mysticism, and dissociation from the enthusiasts among the sectaries: he classed the Quakers with the Ranters or antinomians, the only difference being the indecisive merit of outward holiness in the former.

His first wife died in 1658. She has bequeathed to history only her marriage portion of pious books; even her name is unknown. After 1654 she had borne two more children of whose baptisms, if they took place, there remains no record. He married a second wife, Elizabeth, in 1659. Some impression of her character can be gained from the simple and moving plea she made for her husband two years later, before the judges at the Swan in Bedford, which aroused the pity of the noble Sir Matthew Hale. Bunyan rose rapidly in importance in the congregation, and would have been made a deacon had he not been so constantly "taken off by the preaching of the Gospel".[5] In this period, as he relates in *Grace Abounding*, the terror of guilt was still so near to him that for two years he cried out in his sermons against men's sins: "I went myself in Chains to preach to them in Chains; and carried that Fire in my own Conscience that I persuaded them to beware of."

His next book, *A Few Sighs from Hell, or the Groans of a Damned Soul* (1658) is made up from sermon material of this kind. A royalist wit inserted an advertisement of it in a newspaper immediately after the announcement of the Protector's death. Bunyan mentions in his relation of his imprisonment that he was prepared to show the notes of his sermons to any one who accused him of disloyalty, a statement which would confirm the reader's impression that most of his published treatises were compiled from sermon manuscripts; the numbered heads of reasons and uses, the piecemeal proving of a case by Biblical citations, all suggest that his minor works were transcribed from notes with very little revision. From hellfire preaching he passed naturally to expounding the doctrine of salvation by grace (1658–60). *The Doctrine of the Law and Grace Unfolded* (1659) is the fruit of this period and the most important exposition of his theology; the years of conventicles and experience meetings had provided a severe dialectical

training for the unlettered tinker, who had acquired a remarkable grasp of Calvinist method. Like other seventeenth-century
English Calvinists Bunyan softens the rigours of the doctrine
by drawing attention to the idea of a covenant between God
and his chosen people; he popularizes the idea skilfully.
The Law and Grace also contains some rough sketches of
spiritual autobiography: there is an account of the incident
when a voice from heaven made him pause during his Sunday
sports, and personal experience is drawn on less obtrusively
to explain the perils incident to conversion.

> Also, the soul shall not want enemies, even in its own heart's
> trust, as covetousness, adultery, blasphemy, unbelief, hardness
> of heart, coldness . . . hanging, like so many blocks, at its heels,
> ready to sink into the fire of hell every moment, together with
> strange apprehensions of God and Christ, as if now they were
> absolutely turned to be its enemies, which maketh it doubt of the
> certainty of its salvation. [6]

There is more ease and confidence than in the earlier works.
The general application of the argument is summed up in a
series of questions and answers which anticipates the dialogues
in *The Pilgrim's Progress* in which characters catechize each
other. The style ranges from the quietly familiar, with the
suggestion of a domestic interior, to the flagrantly brutal when
Bunyan in his role of the honest and uneducated lay preacher
is deliberately shocking:

> You know when children fall down in the dirt, they do usually
> before they go home make their clothes as clean as they can, for
> fear their parents should chide them. . . .

> Physicians, you know, if they love to be honoured will not
> bid the patients first make themselves whole, and then come to
> them; no, but bid them come with their sores all running on them,
> as the woman with her bloody issue, Mark v, and as Mary
> Magdalene with her belly full of devils, and the lepers all
> scabbed. . . . [7]

III

The self-consciousness of the mechanic preacher was stimulated by the incessant attacks of university-trained clergy, both Anglican and Presbyterian. In May, 1659, when Bunyan was holding a service in a barn at Toft in Cambridge-shire, he had an encounter with Thomas Smith, Professor of Arabic at Cambridge and University Librarian. Smith questioned his right to preach the gospel, quoting "How shall they preach except they be sent?" and Bunyan replied by saying the church at Bedford had sent him. Smith continued the dispute in print, and was answered by the Baptist Henry Denne, who may have been an old acquaintance of Bunyan: "You seem to be angry with the Tinker because he strives to mend souls as well as Kettles and Pans."[8] A more important Puritan intellectual, William Dell, rector of Yelden, gave Bunyan his protection at this time; after his career as an army chaplain he had become under the Commonwealth Master of Caius College, Cambridge. He allowed the tinker to preach from his pulpit on Christmas Day, 1659, and in consequence some of his parishioners petitioned the House of Lords against him. His brilliant and heterodox mind was intolerant of any man-made distinctions or conditions in church government; he must have exercised a considerable influence over his near neighbours of the Bedford church, and like Bunyan, he was "professedly against *Paedobaptism*, and yet he had his own children baptized".[9]

The ten golden years, in which the separatists had enjoyed freedom and even a measure of authority, were now at an end (only the Quakers suffered badly from persecution in this period). The brief and ineffectual rule of Cromwell's son Richard was succeeded by some months of squabbling between the generals and the remnant of the Long Parliament. Then a new Parliament met which was predominantly royalist, and in May, 1660, Charles II returned to his throne.

Even before the Restoration the Bedford brethren had set apart days of prayer on account of the distractions of the nation. They seem to have expected the worst. Burton had died by September, leaving them without a pastor. Common Prayer was beginning to be reintroduced in the churches; but long before any of the new reign's penal legislation had been enacted, Bunyan, their ablest preacher, was arrested under an old Elizabethan act against conventicles and nonconformity (35 Eliz c.i.).[10] On 12th November at Samsell in south Bedfordshire he was brought before a zealous local magistrate, Francis Wingate; Wingate's estate had suffered in the war and he probably felt he was paying off old scores against the dissenters. Bunyan refused to give an assurance that he would not preach again, and was therefore committed to the county gaol in Bedford. Until the later nineteenth century the local legend that his imprisonment took place in the small town clink on the old bridge was widely accepted. It was however a county offence and would be punished in the county prison. At Quarter Sessions in January 1661 he confronted a bench on which the chief figure was Sir John Keeling, a prominent cavalier lawyer who had been crown counsel at the trial of the regicides and was later to become Lord Chief Justice.

Bunyan's examination before the magistrates is the central event of his active life, and we are fortunate in possessing a detailed narrative of it in his own words (in *A Relation of the Imprisonment of Mr. John Bunyan*). There was some precedent among the sectaries for including verbatim accounts of prosecutions in their autobiographies; they were intent on impressing their public with their witness for the truth, and were conscious of the parallels with the trials of the apostles in the Acts. Bunyan gives an extraordinarily vivid piece of reporting; it has the mark of absolute honesty about it, for the early passages with the magistrates are good humoured and argumentative; a writer who wished to create a literary impression of heroic martyrdom would have slurred over this part, which is in some ways the most interesting. To hear a man like Keeling exchanging scripture arguments with the nonconformist tinker is to be taken inside the seventeenth-century mind. "It is lawful to use Common Prayer and such like forms: for Christ taught his disciples to pray, as John also taught his disciples. . . . Faith comes by hearing." Later when Keeling begins to bluster, Bunyan stands unmoved, abiding by his texts with a pedantic but sublime literalness.

The full extent of his courage may be realized if it is remembered that by a simple undertaking not to preach again to a public assembly he might have obtained his release. He could still have exhorted his fellow church members in private in their houses. Every kind of pressure, ranging from bullying to friendly advice from Wingate's servants, had been brought to bear on him to give such an assurance. He knew beforehand that a constable would visit the meeting at Samsell, and could have postponed it. But he had made up his mind then "if I should fly, it might be a discouragement to the whole body"; he would "go upon the forlorn hope in this country", and be the first to suffer for the gospel. In his ignorance of the law he was even in doubt about the nature of his penalty and at first feared an actual martyrdom. The provisions of the Act were for three months' imprisonment in the first instance, to be followed by transportation if the offender would not then give up preaching and conform to the Established Church; death was only prescribed for a banished felon who returned to England without a pardon. Strictly Bunyan should have been released after three months, and then arrested again if he repeated his crime. After three months a conversation took place in prison with the clerk of the justices, Paul Cobb, who tried to persuade him to submit with much earnest and familiar advice, calling him "neighbour" and "goodman". Cobb's fruitless visit took the place of release and re-arrest, and enabled the justices to keep Bunyan a prisoner while avoiding the responsibility attached to the harsher sentence of transportation. The attitude of the Restoration bench was that sectaries were to be suppressed, not as heretics, but as troublesome disturbers of law and order. For their part the Nonconformists resisted simply for conscience' sake; yet Bunyan whose youth had been spent in an atmosphere of religious revolution, could be not without hope "that my imprisonment might be an awakening to the Saints in the Country". By the "Country" he meant the surrounding region, and the awakening he envisaged may have been a purely spiritual one, but in view of the Bedford church's keen interest in the affairs of the nation under the Protectorate, some not very definite aspiration after a public settlement more favourable to the godly cannot be ruled out. A contributory reason for Bunyan's continued imprisonment was the alarm of the authorities at the outbreak of Fifth Monarchy extremists in London in 1661.

After satisfying his conscience by passive resistance, Bunyan tried to obtain his release. His wife had had a miscarriage on learning of his arrest, and now she and her four step-children had to turn to the charity of friends till he could resume his trade. He was exempted from the Coronation amnesty in April, 1661. At the so-called Midsummer Assizes in August his wife petitioned the justices and finally obtained an interview with them. From all of them except Sir Matthew Hale she received abuse, and to one who said that her husband's doctrine was the doctrine of the devil she replied with dignity "My Lord, when the righteous Judge shall appear, it will be known that his doctrine is not the doctrine of the Devil". Hale pitied her, and advised her to petition the King, or to sue for a pardon, or to obtain a writ of error (much legal ingenuity was expended in that age in finding flaws in the indictment). This latter course was, he said, the cheapest, but since nothing came of it we may assume it was too expensive for Elizabeth Bunyan. Bunyan did however gain in this grim way some legal knowledge which he put to use later: errors in the indictment provide an allegorical device in *The Holy War*. At the Spring Assizes in 1662 he tried to arrange that he might be brought before the judge as a man who had served his sentence and was therefore qualified for release; but the plausible Paul Cobb, possibly acting as agent of the local squirearchy, had his name taken out of the list of felons and stopped his case from coming up.

The circumstances of his imprisonment were less severe than nonconformist martyrology at one time maintained. The county gaol, at the corner of High Street and Silver Street, had its felons' quarters on the ground floor; above where the debtors were housed was a day-room which was used as a chapel. At one period of Bunyan's confinement, there were about sixty dissenters there including two local ministers, "by which means the prison was very much crouded". There was thus opportunity for preaching even in the gaol. The seventeenth-century prisoner depended on what comforts his own and his friends' purses could provide for everything above mere subsistence, and the Bedford deacons may have given some help. Bunyan was able to provide for his family by making "many hundred gross of long Tagg'd Laces"; he also found time to write out many of his discourses for the press. There was no prohibition on visitors; his heroic behaviour and the regular appearance of his books increased his reputation and cases of conscience were brought to him in his cell. A woman from Wellingborough who had stolen from the till of the shop-keeper who employed her came to him to confess. A prisoner's degree of freedom depended much on the whim of his gaoler, and Bunyan seems to have been fortunate, especially in the early days of his imprisonment when he still had hopes of release. He even made journeys to London to solicit the help of Baptists there; and the *Church Book* records that on 28th September, 1661, he was sent with three other brethren to admonish lapsed members. After 26th October his name is not mentioned at the meetings till October, 1668; we may infer that confinement became stricter.

With the Act of Uniformity in 1662 the full tide of persecution fell upon the dissenters. Hundreds of ministers who would not accept the Book of Common Prayer or episcopal ordination were ejected from the livings they had held under the Commonwealth. In 1664 a new and more severe conventicle act was passed which prescribed crippling fines or imprisonment for anyone taking part; the Five Mile Act of 1665 drove the ministers without the city limits and outside their former cures. Not till the expiration of the Conventicle Act in 1668 and the decline of Clarendon's influence was there any relaxation of these measures. The gap of five and a half years in the meetings recorded in the *Church Book* bears eloquent testimony to the disruption of the Bedford community. Brother Harrington was in hiding; Samuel Fenn, the son of John Fenn, after being in and out of prison, was chosen joint pastor with John White-man. After 1668 Bunyan began to come out again on parole; there are no grounds for supposing that he was released in 1666, and then arrested again, as was maintained by his first editor Charles Doe.[11] He took a leading part in visiting and reforming the backsliders, and the over-scrupulous. Humphrey Merrill was

"cut off" or excommunicated for "openly recanting his profession in a General Quarter Sessions", and there were a
number of similar cases to be dealt with. In this period,
however, though the civil power was inactive, nonconformists
could not go about their business without danger of proceedings
from the Archdeacon's court. At any time they could be cited
to appear for non-attendance at the parish church and then
called before Quarter Sessions; Bunyan's second imprisonment
was almost certainly the result of an ecclesiastical prosecution.[12]

Even before his release he was appointed to the pastorate of
the church. The brethren, "after much seeking God by prayer",
ratified their choice on 21st January, 1672.[13] The Declaration
of Indulgence which was signed by the King in the spring
encouraged the Nonconformists in prison, especially the
Quakers, to apply for release. The Quaker pardon, as it was
called, was granted in September, and Bunyan was one of the
few non-Quakers whose names appeared upon it. Meanwhile
the congregation had taken advantage of the new conditions
by buying a barn from one of their members, Josias Ruffhead,
and fitting it out as a meeting-house; Bunyan's name appears
on the indenture of the sale. The application for licences to
preach for twenty-six ministers in Bedfordshire and the
surrounding counties is in his handwriting: he became the
general organizer for the whole area and earned the nickname
of "Bishop Bunyan". Seven neighbouring churches were
intimately associated with Bedford, and their elders were
called from the Bedford congregation at the meeting which
elected Bunyan.

IV

During the first imprisonment Bunyan published his
spiritual autobiography, *Grace Abounding to the Chief of
Sinners* (1666). Though it follows the precedent of many
ministerial narratives, it is the indispensable key to the creative
element in his religious vision. The other most important works
of this period are *Christian Behaviour* (1663) and *The Holy
City* (1665). *Christian Behaviour* belongs to a numerous
category of Puritan manuals of conduct dealing with the

proper relations between fathers and families, and masters and servants. It emphasizes the traditional aspects of Bunyan's thought, especially his conservative views on economics. Proponents of the theory that all Puritans were the ancestors of modern capitalism and never failed to find a godly excuse for the profit motive would gain little support from a study of this text: "when the Lord saith, thou art to provide for thy house, it giveth thee no license to distracting carefulness; neither doth it allow thee to strive to grasp the world in thy heart, or coffers".[14] *The Holy City* interprets the symbolism of the heavenly city described in Revelation. It grew out of a discourse given in the prison chapel; "while I was in the distributing of it", he says, "it so increased in my hand, that of the fragments that we left I gathered up this basketful".[15] For the first time in this work there appear virtues other than popular simplicity and proverbial flavour. There is a poetic glow about the vision which sustains it through patches of expository tedium; in time of oppression the saints can think of triumph, and a tinge of millenarian feeling contributes to the excitement of the writer. The next year, 1666, was associated by many sectaries with the number of the Beast; the temper of the age was changing, and this was perhaps the last occasion on which the devout could look forward to the consummation of all things within their own span of history. Under this stimulus Bunyan's prose assumes a prouder rhythm.

> Never was fair weather after foul—nor warm weather after cold— nor a sweet and beautiful spring after a heavy, and nipping, and terrible winter, so comfortable, sweet, desirable, and welcome to the poor birds and beasts of the field, as this day will be to the Church of God.[16]

Among minor treatises, *I will Pray with the Spirit* (1663) was written against the set forms of the Book of Common Prayer, the indirect reason for his imprisonment. *Profitable Meditations* (1661), *One Thing is Needful* (1664?), and *Prison Meditations* (1665), are his first attempts at verses which are pedestrian but never contemptible.

Most of these early books were published by Francis Smith, known as "Elephant" Smith, who was often in trouble for issuing unlicensed books by dissenters. L'Estrange, Charles II's censor, raided his warehouse near Temple Bar in 1666, and the destruction of much of the confiscated stock in the Great Fire explains the rarity of early Bunyan editions.

In the years immediately before his release Bunyan was involved in two controversies, one with a latitudinarian Anglican divine, Edward Fowler, the other with various London Baptists who insisted on rebaptism by "dipping" as a condition of communion. Bunyan must have obtained books with ease in prison, for he read Fowler's *Design of Christianity* (1670) soon after it came out. Fowler belonged to the new Cambridge school who held an undogmatic view of Christianity and, in violent contrast to the Calvinists, believed that its essence lay in the perfecting of man's moral nature. All Bunyan's natural pugnacity was aroused by reliance on human righteousness, but, as if this was not enough, the author of the offending book was an ejected Nonconformist of 1662 who later conformed and became rector of Northill a few miles from Bedford. In *A Defence of the Doctrine of Justification by Faith* (1672) Bunyan was attacking Fowler's "unstable weathercock spirit" as well as his theology. Much mud was thrown on either side, and not inappropriately Fowler, or his curate, replied in a pamphlet entitled *Dirt Wip'd Off.*

The dispute with the London Baptists was less rancorous and more important. In *A Confession of my Faith and a Reason of my Practice* (1672) Bunyan took his stand for communion on a broad basis with all professing Christians of good repute. A storm of protest arose from the Strict Particular members of his own sect, but the more enlightened wing of the Independents, which included men as hard to label as Henry Jessey and the Oxford scholar, John Tombes, does not seem to have looked on the work unfavourably. Bunyan was continuing the tradition of Gifford and also developing Dell's distinction between spirit-baptism and water-baptism. His liberalism on this question is quite startling when contrasted with the uncompromising theological orthodoxy he had just demonstrated.

As for me, I hope I am a Christian . . . and as for those factious titles of Anabaptists, Independents, and Presbyterians, or the like, I conclude they came neither from Jerusalem nor Antioch, but rather from Hell and Babylon; for they naturally tend to divisions, 'you may know them by their fruits'.[17]

After 1672 Bunyan preached in some London open-communion churches which kept up a connexion with Bedford. George Cokayne, pastor of the meeting in Red Cross Street, became a lifelong friend; he was also associated with Stephen More's church in Winchester Yard, Southwark, and with John Gammon's in Boar's Head Yard. He may have given one of the Tuesday morning lectures against Popery which a group of London merchants had endowed at Pinners' Hall; if so he was ranked with Owen and Baxter, the intellectual giants of Nonconformity.

In the evangelical works published after his release there is some vigorous writing as well as pulpit rhetoric of the cruder sort. *The Barren Fig-tree* (1673) exposes that familiar object of Puritan wrath, the faithless professor; *Light for them that Sit in Darkness* (1675) is written to correct the errors of the Quakers and the problems of the over-scrupulous; *Instruction for the Ignorant* (1675) a catechism for the use of the church, grew out of the communion controversy; *Saved by Grace* and *The Strait Gate* (1675) show an increasing use of fancy and humour in the presentation of the same recurring topics; the reiterated threats and comforts are enlivened by character studies and passages of reported dialogue.

V

It is little wonder that when Bunyan found a more suitable form than the sermon treatise for his human insight and ready store of images, he should have taken, as the main theme of his fiction, a journey along the highway. Many hours of the day must have been spent by him on the indifferent Bedfordshire roads, on saddle or on foot, attending to the needs of his far-flung "diocese". Even beyond its bounds, tradition records preaching forays as far north as Leicester, southwards to Luton and beyond there to the St. Albans neighbourhood,

and eastwards from the daughter church at Gamlingay in
Cambridgeshire to Melbourn near Royston. Oral traditions
were preserved into the nineteenth century, of a great con-
course of people in one place, or, in another, of a trapdoor
used to escape from informers, and still pointed out.

He was too busy to keep regular minutes of the Bedford
meetings, and the entries in the *Church Book* in his handwriting are few and scrappy.[18] They record a good deal of
trouble and opposition; the high standards of the little society
had to be restored after years of disruption, and punishment
meted out to lapsed professors. There was Sister Landey
who taught her children to play cards, and John Rush who
was above the ordinary rate of drunkards, for when carried
home he could not be presented "as one alive to his familie,
he was so dead drunk". More delicate problems were presented
by John Wildman who spread scandal about the ministers,
and Nehemiah Cox, an elder himself and a cordwainer who knew
Greek and Hebrew, and who propagated unorthodox opinions
under the cover of his learning. Bunyan had to be the stern
disciplinarian and inevitably he made enemies. Also, like
other masterful clerical personalities, he could not prevent
women members of his flock from becoming infatuated with
him. This was the case with twenty-one-year-old Agnes Beaumont, who persuaded him to take her behind him on his
horse to a distant meeting, against her father's wishes. Scandal
was already in the air: when her father died suddenly two days
later and a rejected suitor accused her of murder, the situation
looked grim. But a commonsense coroner's inquest cleared
her of the charge and exposed the accuser's malice. The whole
story is told in her remarkable *Narrative*, which also contains
passages of religious rapture suggesting that she had acquired
Bunyan's personal manner of applying verses from the Bible
to each phase of the emotional life.[19]

After the repeal of the Declaration of Indulgence, there was a
renewal of persecution. His old enemies acted as soon as they
could. A warrant against him signed by all the principal county
magistrates was issued on 4th March, 1675; but it seems as
though Bunyan somehow eluded this civil warrant. He was,
however, imprisoned a second time for about six months

before the end of June 1677. He had neglected a summons to appear before the Archdeacon's Court as a nonconformist, and an old enemy, William Foster, Commissary of Bedford, had obtained a writ against him *de excommunicato capiendo* transmitted through Chancery. His powerful friend Owen, the leader of the Independents, applied to Barlow, Bishop of Lincoln, for his release, and two members of Cokayne's congregation entered into a bond for his good behaviour.

Tradition associates the composition of *The Pilgrim's Progress* with the second imprisonment. With its publication in 1678, Bunyan's life ceases to be merely that of a prominent sectary. The book was in the hands of readers of every class all over England and in the New England across the Atlantic, and it was translated before his death into Welsh, French and Dutch. In his last ten years he became a great public figure. Charles II spoke of him to Owen, and his London preaching drew over a thousand to the meeting-house at seven in the morning. His fame gave him the confidence to continue his exploration of the imaginatively freer forms of the religious allegory and the improving novel. *The Life and Death of Mr. Badman* came in 1680; it was followed by *The Holy War* in 1682, and the Second Part of *The Pilgrim's Progress* in 1684. All the time the flow of published sermons did not diminish.

When James II ascended the throne, and after the suppression of Monmouth's rebellion in the west, the last great wave of persecution overtook the dissenters. Fame did not make Bunyan immune from danger. In December 1685 by a deed of gift he transferred all his property to his "well-beloved wife, Elizabeth Bunyan". It was a device to protect his family if he should be imprisoned a third time, and since there was no other trustee named, he would himself retain effective control on his wife's behalf. In a fashion not altogether out of place in that transitional age he combined Puritan heroism with a nonconformist eye to business. His shrewdness was again tested in 1687, when the position had been transformed by James II's plans for conciliating the dissenters in order to win toleration for Catholics. Through his agent, Lord Aylesbury, James tried to woo Bunyan, and even offered him a place, but he refused to be drawn, and contented himself with obtain-

D

ing seats for members of his church on the reorganized corporation of Bedford.

The anonymous biographer who has preserved the story of how Bunyan extricated himself from high politics, has also left an account of his appearance at this period:

> As for his Person he was Tall of Stature, strong boned, though not corpulent somewhat of a Ruddy Face, with sparkling eyes, wearing his hair on his upper lip, after the old British fashion; his Hair Reddish, but in his latter days time had sprinkled it with Grey, his nose well set, but not declining or bending, and his mouth moderate large, his forehead something high, and his habit always plain and modest.[20]

This agrees with the pencil drawing by Robert White, where a face inclined to heaviness is given distinction by the fine nose and the alert, humorous eyes.

He died in harness. On one of his preaching journeys to London, he went out of his way to Reading to patch up a quarrel between father and son. After riding through heavy rain, he arrived soaked through at the house of a London friend. He was able to preach on the following Sunday, but in a few days a violent fever developed. He died on 31st August, 1688, and was buried in Bunhill Fields.

NOTES

CHAPTER II

The principal sources for Bunyan's biography are his own account in *Grace Abounding* (the 6th ed. of 1688 is the fullest) and in *A Relation of the Imprisonment of Mr. John Bunyan* (1765), *The Continuation of Mr. Bunyan's Life* (in *Grace Abounding*, 7th ed. 1692, pp. 157–71), and Charles Doe's *The Struggler* in the first folio ed. of Bunyan's *Works* in 1692. The latter contains the first Bunyan bibliography.

There is a facsimile ed. of the *Church Book of Bunyan Meeting* with an introduction by G. B. Harrison (1928). The original is in the Bunyan Library at Bedford.

The most authoritative modern life is still that of John Brown, *John Bunyan: his Life, Times, and Work*, in the revised ed. by F. M. Harrison (1928).

1. *Church Book*, pp. 1–4, give an account of the founding of the church, and the testament of Gifford, its first pastor.

2. Brown, *John Bunyan*, pp. 82–3.

3. It was printed in *The Humble and Serious Testimony of many hundreds of godly and well affected people in the county of Bedford* (1657). Similar debates on the position of the Protector took place in Dr. Peter Chamberlen's Lothbury church which was Baptist and Fifth Monarchy: see its minute book in the Bodleian, Rawlinson MS. D828, F. 33a. An earlier Bedford petition of 1653 has a Bunyan signature which is disputable (Brown, *John Bunyan*, pp. 122–3).

4. For the controversy with Burrough, see W. C. Braithwaite, *The Beginnings of Quakerism* (1932), pp. 285–8, and Elisabeth Brockbank, *Edward Burrough, a Wrestler for Truth, 1634–62* (1949), pp. 105–9.

5. *Church Book*, p. 19.

6. *The Doctrine of the Law and Grace Unfolded*, in *The Works of John Bunyan* edited by George Offor (1860–2), I, p. 546.

7. *Op. cit.*, I, p. 556.

8. Henry Denne, *The Quaker No Papist* (1659), A2.

9. *Calamy Revised*, ed. A. G. Matthews (1934), p. 162.

10. For Bunyan's imprisonments, see W. T. Whitley, *Transactions of the Baptist Historical Society*, vi (1918–19), pp. 1–24, W. G. Thorpe, *Proceedings of the Society of Antiquaries*, 2nd Series, xii, pp. 11–17, and Joyce Godber, *Transactions of the Congregational Historical Society*, Vol. XVI, No. 1 (April 1949).

11. Charles Doe, *The Life and Death of Mr. John Bunyan, late Minister of the Gospel at Bedford* (appended to *The Heavenly Footman*, 1698).

12. See Miss Godber's article cited above on the bond for his release found in the Buckingham Archdeaconry records and now in the Aylesbury Museum.

13. *Church Book*, pp. 50–1.

14. *Christian Behaviour* (Offor, *Works*, II, p. 557).

15. Offor, *Works*, III, p. 398.

16. Offor, *Works*, III, p. 409.

17. *Peaceable Principles and True* (Offor, *Works*, II, p. 649).

18. *Church Book*, pp. 53–72.

19. *The Narrative of the Persecution of Agnes Beaumont in 1674*, ed. with an Introduction by G. B. Harrison (1929).

20. *The Continuation of Mr. Bunyan's Life*, pp. 170–1.

SPIRITUAL AUTOBIOGRAPHY

"HERE are Sixty Pieces of his Labours, and he was Sixty Years of age," writes Charles Doe, Bunyan's first editor and biographer, as he introduces the first bibliography of his hero's works, which he appended to the second edition of *The Heavenly Footman*. Most of these sixty books are moral and doctrinal treatises of the conventional Puritan pattern. They are the stock-in-trade of the popular preacher, sermons and commentaries on Scripture, worked up into a more formal shape, with numbered heads of doctrines and applications. Both the construction of these homilies and the quality of their religious exhortation are little different from those of other Nonconformists of the period. Again and again Bunyan preaches the plight of fallen human nature, utterly divorced from the power and goodness of God, and unable to help itself. Then he follows his exposition of the terrors of the old Law by pointing to the consolation of the Gospel with its offer of the free grace of Christ. This alternation of terror and comfort is the systole and diastole of Bunyan's religious thought. In *Sighs from Hell* he concludes the most appalling account of the pains of the damned with "A few considerations of encouragement".[1] And his controversial pamphlets against Quakers and Latitudinarians are directed against beliefs which threatened to obscure the Calvinist distinction between grace and nature. All these treatises follow the traditional practice of the Puritan popular sermon; the modern reader is perhaps more likely to be repelled by the form than by the theology: there is a wearisome iteration of numbered objections and answers, and this appearance of logical structure is not in harmony with the essentially emotional approach to dogma.

But the style is Bunyan's own; the rough texture of his prose is lightened by passionate conviction, by imagination and humour, and above all by a fund of realistic imagery drawn from the life of the people. Other "mechanick preachers" might cultivate such imagery, and a similar rhetoric of emphatic repetition, but none comes near to Bunyan. The reason is that there is nothing self-conscious about his rusticity. Many of the other artisan preachers are acutely class-conscious; they see themselves as the elect who have been preferred by God before the rich and learned; they exploit their lack of education to the utmost, and emphasize their kinship with apostolic Christianity with somewhat too intellectual an assurance. In contrast, Bunyan draws quite naturally on common life and the culture of the countryside: in expounding the Gospel he can echo the very tones of the parables, because he has grown up close to the soil in an agricultural community. He compares the small number of the elect to the gleanings in harvest:

> What are the gleanings to the whole crop? and yet you here see, to the gleanings are the saved compared. . . . You know it is often the cry of the poor in harvest, Poor gleaning, poor gleaning.[2]

Or, as he enumerates the different sacrifices which constitute Christ's love for men, the formal catalogue is brightened by the phrase: "He became poorer than they that go with flail and rake." His comparisons always elucidate his moral message; they appeal to common experience and bring reader and writer nearer together, in contexts where any suggestion of a literary flourish would draw them apart:

> Poor coming soul, thou art like a man that would ride full gallop, whose horse will hardly trot! Now the desire of his mind is not to be judged by the slow pace of the dull jade he rides, but by the hitching and kicking and spurring as he sits on his back.

The immediacy of this image presents the reader with a part of his own everyday life seen in a new light as the type of the eternal. It might be said of Bunyan, as it was of his fellow-Baptist, Benjamin Keach:

> He's a popular Preacher, and (as appears by his awakening Sermons) understands the Humour and necessity of his audience.[3]

But Bunyan's understanding of his audience springs from a real sympathy with its more inarticulate members; it is quite different from a rhetorician's cold-blooded attempt to play upon the feelings.

However, when the most generous allowance has been made for the qualities of style in the sermons, it is idle to pretend that the general reader will turn to them for any intrinsic reasons. Bunyan's reputation outside his own climate of opinion is grounded upon only four of the sixty books in Doe's catalogue. These are two masterpieces of religious literature, *Grace Abounding* and *The Pilgrim's Progress*; and two notable books of a second order of genius, *The Life and Death of Mr. Badman* and *The Holy War*. *Grace Abounding* is far more than a valuable document for illustrating Bunyan's spiritual development: in it he begins to struggle with the language at his command in order to evolve from it forms suitable for the expression of his inner experience. Because he must tell others of his temptations and the assurance of salvation which followed them, he has to create each experience anew in the most powerful and physically evocative phrases: he has to become, in spite of his Puritan self, a literary artist. In a bitter struggle to make the simple words he knew, descriptive of physical action, convey the nameless terrors and joys of his inner life, he began to shape the contents of his imagination into palpable forms. Already he has gone part of the way towards an allegorical fiction in which psychological phenomena are endowed with a life of their own. When Bunyan came to write *The Pilgrim's Progress* he had only to translate his spiritual odyssey into an allegory.

If it had not been for his long imprisonment between 1660 and 1672 neither work might have been written. We might only have had "Bishop Bunyan", the energetic, extraverted popular preacher, entirely absorbed in evangelism and the direction of souls. For he seems to have emerged from the years of despair preceding his conversion a new man: his faith released him from morbid introspection; the massive strength of mind which had been divided against itself was now integrated and applied, efficiently and courageously, to the affairs of the Bedford separatist church. His conscience, so sickly in the matter of his own salvation, resolutely refused the slightest compromise when he came into conflict with the civil power. But prison drove him back upon himself. He was suddenly cut off from the world of other people in which he had begun to move so confidently. The cause of his isolation lay in the very religious experience which had integrated his personality and given him new life. Inevitably the situation invited him to review the period of introspection which had culminated in his conversion; he had to measure the length and breath of the faith that sustained him, and as a Protestant that meant that he had to explore his own inner condition. His faith was not again subjected to doubt, but it was incumbent on him to give an account of himself and God's dealings with him that would comfort the brethren outside prison, now deprived of his immediate guidance.

Thus one of the deepest impulses of Bunyan's nature, his desire for wholeness and health of mind, was called into play in the composition of *Grace Abounding*. Yet the form of the book and much of its matter are not unique. It belongs to a large class of spiritual autobiographies written by seventeenth-century Puritans, and the form was especially cultivated after 1640 by leaders of the more radical sects. The tendency of Puritanism to make the regeneration of the individual soul the central fact of religious experience encouraged the keeping of diaries and the compilation of minute accounts of conversion. Conversion was regarded, as we have seen, not as a sudden change, but as a gradual process marked by certain clearly defined stages. There was the first intimation of grace, often received in a sermon, then conviction of sin, when the Christian began to see that his righteousness was but "filthy rags", and then a series of assurances from God leading to effectual calling. This last was the final token of election; he then knew that he was numbered with those at the right hand of Christ, through no merits of his own but through Christ's righteousness imputed to him. As the New Englander, Samuel Williard, said, God's decree of election may run "under ground a great while before it rise and break out in effectual Calling".[4] Hence the need for constant self-examination. Though the general pattern was the same, the symptoms of grace in the soul might differ from one person to another; study and comparison were necessary. Professor Perry Miller remarks that "the art of biography as understood by the Puritans was the preparation of case-histories";[5] and the habit of the diary in which a man may confront himself each day was bequeathed to us by the Puritans.

This Puritan biography grew up among the academic Puritans before the Civil Wars. Often it took the form of the funeral panegyric, as in Thomas Taylor's *Profitable Memoriall of the Conversion of Mrs. Marie Gunter* (1633). When a prominent minister's works were published it became customary to prefix to them a short life by one of his friends; and sometimes a minister's autobiographical memoranda would reach the public. Those of Thomas Goodwin relate some of the classic crises of conversion, found again in Bunyan and others; there is, for instance, the awakening of his sense of sin by a sermon.[6] The spiritual autobiography assumed a new function and received fresh vitality in the hands of the extreme sectaries between 1640 and 1660. These men were without formal education for the ministry or any official sanction of their right to preach; to establish their claims they had to make clear their special calling, and to do this entailed a more searching inquiry into the work of grace upon them than even the older Puritans had practised. In their hands the autobiography becomes an instrument to justify their claims and to convert others. These narratives usually fall into three divisions: conversion, calling and ministry. The first two divisions are only concerned with the external events of a man's life in so far as they reveal the subterranean current of God's dealings with him.

This tendency to dwell upon the continuous, impalpable life of the mind has much in common with the method of modern literary introspection. However, the complete neglect of the ordinary history of a person may seem strange to us. Bunyan makes one tantalizingly vague reference to the period of his military service in the county levy, and only does so to illustrate a special providence of God towards him:

When I was a soldier, I, with others, were drawn out to go to such a place to besiege it; but when I was just ready to go, one of the Company desired to go in my Room; to which when I had consented, he took my Place; and coming to the Siege, as he stood Sentinel, he was shot into the head with a musket bullet, and died.

But we can understand the importance granted to the imponderables of individual psychology, since the Puritan method of analysis has entered into the tradition of autobiography. The word "experience" came to be used in the later seventeenth century to denote "a state of mind or feeling forming part of the inner religious life; the mental history (of a person) with regard to religious emotion".[7] There was in the gathered churches, both in England and New England, the institution of the experience-meeting at which believers compared their spiritual states; in some congregations, including that of Bedford, new converts were obliged to testify to their calling before the whole meeting. The self-awareness of the Puritan was sharpened by these ordeals of analysis. The idea of personal providences and the belief that the process of sanctification should be extended to the smallest details of thought and behaviour made every aspect of consciousness interesting; later, when the theological drive that inspired this psychological interest had slackened, the apparatus of analysis, now completely secularized, still persisted: "experience" of any kind is now interesting if it assists the personality in its task of self-exploration. The shadow of the Puritan method hangs over the self-examinations of Defoe's and Richardson's heroines, over the less edifying pages of Boswell's *Journal*, and over the perverse sincerity and unquiet conscience of Gide.

It would therefore be wrong to conclude that an outmoded theology sets up a barrier between Bunyan's autobiography and ourselves. The extreme self-consciousness of the method is modern and post-Cartesian; as for the subject-matter, though Bunyan gives special theological names to his terrors, and sees them as the work of a personal devil, they share with modern neuroses the general character of anxiety. Nagging anxiety and the uneasy conscience recommend Bunyan for consideration as a cousin of the modern man. His religious development can easily be studied as a psychiatric case-history showing a progress from severe maladjustment (accompanied by hallucinations and paronoiac symptoms) to a

successful integration of the personality. But this would be to
approach no nearer to the secret of the book. It would simply
be to translate the psychological terminology of the seventeenth
century into that of the twentieth. Why does Bunyan's narrative
exercise a peculiar fascination over the reader, while the
closely parallel accounts of their religious experience by his
Baptist contemporaries do not? Behind his terminology there is a
greater depth of religious sensibility which transcends the
bounds of the particular language of religious opinion he
shared with his fellow-Baptists, and allies him with great
converts in other communions.

The Puritan psychology of conversion provided a mould
ready to receive the experience of the believer; the conventional pattern had been established by numerous cases: it was
customary, for instance, for the tender conscience of the
convert to dwell upon the venial sins of his unregenerate life.
Bunyan tells us that:

> until I came to the State of Marriage, I was the very Ringleader
> of all the Youth that kept me company, in all manner of vice and
> ungodliness.
> Yea, such prevalency had the Lusts and Fruits of the Flesh
> in this poor Soul of mine, that, had not a Miracle of precious
> Grace prevented, I had not only perished by the Stroke of eternal
> Justice, but had also laid myself open even to the Stroke of those
> Laws, which bring some to Disgrace and open Shame before the
> Face of the World.

In spite of the last statement, it seems likely that here he
was much exaggerating the magnitude of his sins of the flesh.
The writings suggest a masculine and passionate nature; he
married early, but there is little evidence for a period of
youthful promiscuity like that of St. Augustine, tempting as
it might be to multiply parallels between *Grace Abounding*
and the *Confessions*. On the other hand, there was a contemporary habit of exaggeration in these matters. Time that was
wasted in venial sins or mere idleness seemed almost as terrible
a loss to God as time spent in grave misdoing. Cromwell had
no period of shameful depravity to look back on, but he could
say:

Blessed be his name for shining upon so dark a heart as mine! You know what my manner of life hath been. Oh, I lived in and loved darkness, and hated light; I was a chief, the chief of sinners. This is true; I hated godliness, yet God had mercy on me. O the riches of his mercy![8]

In the light of this it does not seem possible to deduce from Bunyan's rather vague confessions any more than that he was a prominent member of a group of wild and idle young men, that he was given to swearing, and that he indulged in sports on the Sabbath. Because it had become general practice to declaim against the sin of pastimes in a narrative of religious experience, many writers, without necessarily falling into hypocrisy, give a mechanical account of such incidents. Vavasor Powell, the Welsh Baptist, recounts similar incidents and providences to those in Bunyan's story; but he cannot inform his prose with any sense of emotional disturbance; he writes with a mere assent of the will to the commonly accepted scheme of a convert's progress as he had heard·it expounded in a hundred sermons. A man can only give what he has, to God or to literature, and the greater dignity and imaginative resource of Bunyan's nature appear most clearly in passages where the experience is closely paralleled in Powell or other lesser writers. Powell deals thus with a personal providence involving the help afforded by an older spiritual writer:

> At this time the Lord visited me with a very sore and great pain of the tooth-ache . . . and by another good providence I met with a little book of Mr. Perkins, and in that, with this expression, if the pains of one little bone, or tooth, be so grievous for a few days, what then will the pains of the whole body and soul be in hell for evermore? Upon this my terrour began in Conscience to that degree, that it made the other pain to seem somewhat more easier. . . .[9]

The trivial incident of the tooth-ache remains trivial in spite of the attempt to give it eternal significance, and Powell had to get his idea from another man. Bunyan describes with much more art his encounter with an old religious book, the

Elizabethan translation of Luther's *Commentary on Galatians*:

> But before I had got thus far out of these my Temptations, I did greatly long to see some ancient godly Man's experience, who had writ some hundreds of years before I was born. . . . Well, after many such longings in my mind, the God in whose hands are all our days and ways, did cast into my hand, one day, a Book of *Martin Luther*; it was his Comment on the *Galatians*—it also was so old that it was ready to fall piece from piece if I did but turn it over . . . the which, when I had but a little way perused, I found my condition, in his experience, so largely and profoundly handled, as if his Book had been written out of my heart.

Bunyan's dramatic imagination made something of his own from the comfort he found in Luther's book. At a time when he could still fear that the promises of salvation were not for him, he read in it:

> Also they know that they have *an everlasting righteousness*, which they wait for through hope, as a certain and sure possession *laid up for them in heaven*, even when they feele the horrible terrours of sinne and death. . . .[10]

When the moment of exaltation came in which his lingering doubts were finally scattered, this passage returned to him and he seemed to hear Christ speaking in similar words:

> But one day as I was passing in the field, and that too with some dashes on my Conscience, fearing lest all was not right, suddenly this sentence fell upon my soul, *Thy righteousness is in Heaven.*

Likewise, Bunyan relates his morbid terror about the bell-ringing, which had once delighted him, far more convincingly than Powell does his anecdote about tooth-ache. First he feared one of the bells might fall, but still wished to continue as a spectator of his beloved pastime; so he stood under the main beam. But then he began to think that the bell might fall with a swing, and hit him in rebounding from the wall. So he did not dare to come any nearer than the church-door; but then he thought, "How if the *Steeple* itself should fall?" The whole story of this bell-ringing and of other nervous obsessions is put before one with a simplicity that looks through the incidents to the tortured intensity of his mind; yet the incidents are given a firm outline; Bunyan carries his agonies about in the real world, and a slight touch can convey a background or a scene. Once in Bedford "I came where there were three or four poor *Women* sitting at a door in the Sun, and talking about the things of God; and being now willing to hear them discourse I drew near to hear what they said." His visual imagination seized upon their being "in the sun", and remembered it later when he had a dream about the godly people of Bedford; he dreamed they were warm on the sunny side of a mountain while he was kept in frost and snow on the other.

Grace Abounding is, then, the greatest of the Puritan spiritual autobiographies because its exploitation of the providences behind familiar, everyday things is never trivial. Through the introspective method, which was the great contribution of this tradition of analysis, Bunyan has something of substance to reveal. His complete sincerity in personal revelation and the simple directness of his style are aspects of the same integrity. He says in the preface that he could have "stepped into a Style much higher than this in which I have here Discoursed, and could have adorned all things more than here I have seemed to do". He was thinking of the elliptical, biblical style sometimes favoured by the Baptists; he uses it himself in the same preface: there he exhibits the peculiar jargon of radical Puritan piety ("Hungerings and Thirstings also after further Acquaintance with the Father") and the allusions to Scripture ("I have sent you here enclosed a drop of that Honey, that I have taken out of the Carcase of a Lion"); he uses this later, very sparingly, in *The Pilgrim's Progress*, but here, he says, the devil did not play in tempting him, he did not play when he sank as into a bottomless pit, so he may not play now in relating his experiences, but must be "plain and simple, and lay down the thing as it was". When in later editions he added some providential incidents that he had not previously mentioned, we may suspect that he was working over comparatively slight impressions with a view to the conventional pattern of conversion, and, of course, to the missionary value of his book. But the hard core of the narrative is sheer naked self-revelation; naturally, the stages which correspond to the ideal mould of a Calvinist conversion are thrown into a high light, but the depth of Bunyan's feelings, whether of love or terror, go beyond the inspiration of a particular system of theology:

> I thought I could have spoken of his Love, and of his Mercy to me, even to the very Crows that sat upon the plowed Lands before me.

He presents one of the classical examples of a "twice-born" conversion, and in the comparative infancy of modern psychology William James recorded the symptoms of his case. But to turn from a theological to a psychological system of pigeon-holing does not help us to understand the real inwardness of that case. We may say that he was "a victim of verbal automatisms, both motor and sensory", but something is lost, once we exchange Bunyan's beliefs for any translation into purely psychological terms which neglects their devotional content. He had been haunted even in his boyhood by terrible dreams and his temptations to despair in the period 1648–52 bordered on hallucination; but though his morbid mental condition provided a form of expression for his religious life, it would be a fatal over-simplification to conclude that his conversion was a matter of pathology. It seems to be a necessary condition for our appreciation of religious genius that we should recognize its aspirations after the divine, though they may be expressed in forms and language remote from our own, as being somehow related to our most intimate everyday feelings about good and evil. The saints and mystics are not psychopathological cases, each enclosed in a private universe of illusion, nor even delightful eccentrics. Bunyan's good and evil are our good and evil, however harsh and strange the shapes of damnation and election which his vision assumes. What does mark him off is the plunge into faith that he makes.

He describes how for a time he lives a "legal" life of outward moral conformity, and gives up his swearing and sports on the Sabbath. His neighbours are impressed by this apparent reformation, but Bunyan soon realizes that this is mere respectability and not religion. The poor women of Bedford, whom he found sitting in the sun, are members of John Gifford's gathered congregation. He hears talk of the new birth and free grace, and begins to attach himself to these people. This is the period when the personality of Gifford, the ex-officer and reformed rake, must have affected him deeply. His understanding of the imperfections of his nature grows. He experiences a temporary gift of grace, prompted by a chance passage in a sermon, but from then on his spirit is in the throes. He yearns for assurance:

> Oh! how I now loved those words that spake of a Christian's calling! As when the Lord said to one, Follow me; and to another, Come after me: and oh, thought I, that he would say so to me too: how gladly would I run after him.

But he is now assaulted by "a very great storm" of temptation. Certain texts of Scripture concerning reprobation and betrayal ring in his ears; they seem to be aimed at him personally, and in the pages of the autobiography they continue to ring out a melancholy refrain. "Simon, Simon, Satan hath desired to have thee," is one of these cries. Even after he seems to have been convinced of his effectual calling, the worst attacks of spiritual despair are still in store for him. For he writes: "I was persuaded that those who were once effectually in Christ, as I hoped, through his Grace, I had seen myself, could never lose him for ever . . .", and is then plunged in a second wave of temptations of doubt, which he speaks of as lasting two and a half years. This was in accordance with the most authoritative Puritan teaching on the work of the Devil; the faithful were more grievously tempted than others in order to try their spiritual endurance. The climax of this second period of mental agony was when Bunyan thought he had committed the sin against the Holy Ghost by denying Christ. Voices whispering "Sell him, sell him", sounded in his ears until with a wrench of the spirit he found himself saying, "Let him go". And then for months he was haunted by the terrible music of the seventeenth verse of the twelfth chapter of the Epistle to the Hebrews:

"For ye know how that afterward, when he would have inherited the blessing, he was rejected, for he found no place of repentance, though he sought it carefully with tears."

At last this period of mental torture gives way to his final assurance of grace. He realizes that the nightmare of his last temptation was really an illusion: in his youthful ignorance as a believer he had not understood the potency of the promises already given. His deepest being was already grounded on God. After undergoing "a great cloud of darkness" accompanied by physical weakness, he reaches the highest pitch of exaltation. He has a vision of the whole company of the saints passing over into the New Jerusalem, which looks forward to the closing scenes of the Second Part of *The Pilgrim's Progress*, when the pilgrims cross the river. Included in this vision is a passage from the same chapter of the Hebrews which had served as a focus for his worst anxieties.

In Bunyan's spiritual sickness the extreme Protestant idea of the Bible as the Word of God was always present to him. Like the majority of Puritan Englishmen of his day, he believed that each verse of the Bible, taken out of its context, still held a message of truth. The fanatics of the sectarian left wing believed that a single text, met at a certain point in time, might have a special message for an individual.[11] The sermon habit, and the tendency to draw providential lessons from the scriptures commented on in a sermon, encouraged this belief. Bunyan's treatment of the Bible reflects the extreme viewpoint; he shows his kinship with the Quakers, who were his bitter rivals as popular evangelists, by interpreting all his texts as if they applied to the condition of the individual soul. When his fear of having committed the unforgiveable sin of betrayal reduces him to a state of physical suffering ("a clogging and heat at my stomach . . . as if my breast-bone would have split asunder"), he thinks of the death of Judas as recorded in the Acts as being directly applicable to him: "Judas, who, by his falling headlong, burst asunder, and all his bowels gushed out." Here we see the remarkable way in which the tradition of bibliolatry harmonized with the psychological temperament of Bunyan, so abnormal in its subjection to verbal automatisms.[12] In the grasp of his powerfully concrete imagination, the quotations from

Scripture are, even within the limits of autobiography, on the way to becoming personified. There are no abstract ideas in *Grace Abounding*; his notions about justification always take on a sensuous life; his theological doubts are expressed as a battle between friendly and hostile texts, and the battlefield is not his mind or his emotions, but his flesh and bones, quaking, sweating and burning by the agency of anxieties which have developed into physical illness.

The metaphors are not illustrative imagery but express the quality of these quasi-physical struggles. There is always not far off a sensation of forcing or pushing, whether it be pushing away evil presences, or unwillingly resisting the Word of God:

I have found my Unbelief to set, as it were, the shoulder to the door to keep him out, and that too even then, when I have with many a bitter sigh cried, *Good Lord, break it open.*

Then there is the beautiful simile in which he compares himself to a child carried off by a gipsy, kicking and struggling as he is borne away "from Friend and Country" under her apron. Here the personal obsession, expressed through the idea of muscular activity, is combined with an image drawn from the lore and experience of the countryside. In a metaphysical religious poet it would seem a delightfully quaint piece of conscious audacity; in Bunyan it is natural and inevitable, like so much of the rural wisdom that mellows his piety.

In the discovery of imagery which is built out of the experience he is trying to describe, Bunyan conforms to a particular type of mystical mentality. The temptations which oppress him resemble the spiritual dryness experienced by the mystic at a certain stage of his progress towards the divine love, when he has detached himself from the creatures; Catholic authorities on mental prayer would be in agreement on this point with the Puritan handbooks of moral theology.[13] But in spite of one or two passages which seem to describe moments of ecstasy, *Grace Abounding* is not a record of gradual progress towards spiritual union with God. Bunyan's primary concern with salvation, rather than union, prevents him from taking the direction of the mystic. The concrete character of his internal

E

experience is never complicated by any metaphysical element;
he does not use the concrete images to make intelligible another
dimension of experience, as a St. Teresa or a St. John of the
Cross employ their erotic imagery. He never passes beyond the
earthy and immediate; however much as a Puritan he may have
neglected certain aspects of the Incarnation, for him indeed the
Word was always made flesh. "That sentence fell upon me,"
"That piece of a sentence darted in upon me." In his moments
of illumination, God makes the Scriptures "shine before me . . .
dwell with me, talk with me, and comfort me". Tactile images
predominate over the figures dependent on other bodily senses.[14]
This is the chief constituent of the harsh concreteness of style.
The physical sense of the strain between the tempter and the
tempted is reproduced in the vocabulary:

> This sentence lay like a mill-post upon my back. . . .
> That scripture did also tear and rend my soul. . . .
> These places did pinch me very sore. . . .
> These thoughts would so confound me, and imprison me, and
> tie me up from faith.

When tormented by the sentence "Simon, Simon, Satan hath
desired to have you" (Luke, xxii, 31), the auditory illusion was
so strong that he would look over his shoulder to see if some
man had actually called:

> I thought verily, as I have told you, that somebody had called
> after me, that was half a Mile behind me; and although that was
> not my Name, yet it made me suddenly look behind me, believing
> that he who called so loud meant me.

The texts which threaten become personified as actual devils
and tormentors; they are ready to take their place as evil
spirits in the Valley of the Shadow of Death, where we shall
eventually re-encounter them.

It is fitting that, in most modern editions, *Grace Abounding*
is concluded by *A Relation of My Imprisonment*. This work was
handed down in manuscript in Bunyan's family and remained
unpublished until 1765. But the imprisonment was a continuation of the ministry, since it was a further witnessing to his

beliefs, and therefore forms an appropriate final section to the spiritual autobiography, according to the traditional division of such works. There is an artistic appropriateness, too. After emerging from the struggles he had described, Bunyan put away entirely his morbid anxieties. He had not only a new birth, but a new personality. Decisively oriented towards the outer world, he was now quite ready to face real enemies without flinching. But his new strength was not inhuman; again his sincerity is complete: he does not gloss over the pain of parting with his family to magnify the courage grace had given him:

> I found myself a man, and compassed with Infirmities. The parting with my Wife and poor Children hath often been to me in this place as the pulling of the Flesh from my Bones; and that not only because I am somewhat too fond of these great Mercies, but also because I should have often brought to my mind the many hardships . . . my poor Family was like to meet with.

In this parting with his family, at the end of his spiritual development, Bunyan found material later for the beginning of his great work. Christian, at the start of his pilgrimage, has to put wife and children behind him. This is the first of many links between the allegory and *Grace Abounding*.

Throughout his autobiography can be felt at work the impulse towards a complete picture of the self; Bunyan sets everything down; he must take a firm grasp on his own being. Without ever straying outside the accepted forms of Puritan edification, the whole book is the expression of this imperious inner need.

NOTES

CHAPTER III

1. Bunyan, *Works*, ed. George Offor (1860–2), III, p. 705.
2. *Works*, ed. Offor, I, p. 380.
3. *The Life and Errors of John Dunton* (1705), p. 236.
4. Samuel Willard, *Mercy Magnified on a Penitent Prodigal*, A3 recto.
5. Perry Miller and T. H. Johnson, *The Puritans* (New York, 1938), p. 461.
6. Thomas Goodwin, *Works* (1704), V, v-xix, cf. Samuel Clarke, *The Lives of Thirty-Two English Divines* (3rd ed. 1677), p. 328.

7. *New English Dictionary*, s. v. Experience, 4b.

8. *Letters and Speeches of Oliver Cromwell*, ed. Thomas Carlyle (Everyman ed.). To Mrs. St. John, I, pp. 81–2.

9. *The Life and Death of Mr. Vavasor Powell* (1671), p. 4.

10. Luther, *A Commentary on the Epistle to the Galatians* (1575), Folio 233.

11. Cf. Samuel Howe, *The Sufficiency of the Spirit's Teaching* (8th ed. 1792), p. 39, where the text "He would cause to perish and destroy the wisdom of the wise" (Isaiah, xxix, 14) is used as an argument against academic qualifications for the clergy.

12. Cf. William James, *Varieties of Religious Experience* (1903), pp. 157 ff.

13. Cf. Edward Leen, *Progress through Mental Prayer* (1938), pp. 115–17, and William Ames, *De Conscientia* (Amsterdam, 1630), Lib. ii, cap. vii, "*De Tentationibus*".

14. Cf. E. Marcault, *Le Cas Bunyan et le tempérament psychologique* (Clermont-Ferrand, 1910), who gives the following proportions:

Tactile imagery	...	40	Visual ...	... ...	11
Auditory	... ...	13	Gustatory	... ...	4

THE ALLEGORY OF THE SOUL

I. The Origins and Composition of *The Pilgrim's Progress*

THE First Part of *The Pilgrim's Progress* was entered in the Stationers' Register on 22nd December, 1677; the Term Catalogues record that it was licensed in the following February. The bookseller was Nathaniel Ponder, of "the Peacock in the Poultry, near Cornhill", destined to be known in the book trade as "Bunyan Ponder". He had not previously published a book by Bunyan, but many Nonconformist works had appeared under his imprint, including those of John Owen, who had been concerned in Bunyan's release from prison. The first edition is remarkable for irregular spellings, loose grammar, and colloquial forms; if this is because it was printed from Bunyan's uncorrected manuscript, it would suggest that other works of his received considerable stylistic revision before reaching the printer. As well as introducing more correct but duller grammar, later editions omit the delightful marginal comments which are to be found in the first: in phrases like "O brave Talkative", "Hopeful swaggers", and "O good riddance", Bunyan expresses keen appreciation of the progress of his own story. Some important passages were added in the second and third editions, most of them expanding the character studies of the allegorical personages met along the road. Among these additions were the whole episode of Mr. Worldly Wiseman, the description of Mr. By-Ends's relations, and the account of Diffidence, the wife of Giant Despair.

The success of the book was immediate. Two more editions appeared within a year, and in 1684 when Bunyan announced his Second Part he could boast that the work had entered every country and every company:

> *My* Pilgrim's *Book has travell'd Sea and Land,*
> *Yet could I never come to understand,*

That it was slighted, or turned out of Door
By any Kingdom, were they Rich or Poor. . . .
If you draw nearer home, it will appear
My Pilgrim, knows no ground of shame, or fear;
City, and Country will him entertain.

The man who was now to enter on his inheritance of fame had
lately been a criminal, according to the laws against Dissenters,
and a prisoner. *The Pilgrim's Progress* is a prison book, like
Boethius's *Consolation of Philosophy*; both works owe their
motive force to an heroic assertion of the inner man against the
blind injustice of confinement. The body becomes dehumanized,
a thing done to, and in compensation the spirit creates a world
of its own. Philosophy descends in palpable form to Boethius's
cell and Evangelist confronts Bunyan, who begins his book:

> As I walk'd through the wilderness of this world, I lighted on a
> certain place, where was a Den; and I laid me down in that place
> to sleep: and as I slept I dreamed a Dream.

The Den is glossed in the margin "The Gaol" in the
seventh edition. But when during his two imprisonments did
Bunyan write the work? He was in prison from 1660 to 1672, and
again for about six months in 1677. There was a strong local
tradition that the place of his imprisonment was the town-clink
on Bedford Bridge; John Brown was the first to see that the
twelve years' confinement, on a warrant signed by the county
justices, must have been in the county gaol, but he still maintained that the short second imprisonment was on the bridge,
and that there a good third of *The Pilgrim's Progress* was written,
up to the point when Bunyan says, for no apparent reason,
"So I awoke from my dream. And I slept, and dreamed
again. . . ."[1] Brown considered that this break in the narrative
marked his release from prison. He also believed that the
second imprisonment was in 1675–6, and that therefore Bunyan
had time to put the work by, and then take it up again and finish
it for the printer by the end of 1677. But the bond has now come
to light for Bunyan's release in June 1677, and it shows that
the second imprisonment also must have been in the county
gaol.[2]

The evidence is scanty, and it does not seem safe to assume that the book was written in the second period in prison and not in the first. The only other piece of internal evidence is in the prefatory verses, "The Author's Apology for his Book". He says:

> When at the first I took my Pen in hand,
> Thus for to write; I did not understand
> That I at all should make a little Book,
> In such a mode . . .
> . . . I writing of the Way
> And Race of Saints, in this our Gospel-Day,
> Fell suddenly into an Allegory
> About their Journey and the way to Glory.

He laid the work by lest it should keep him from the book in hand about "the Race of Saints". If we could be sure which of his minor treatises Bunyan is describing here, it would give us a clue not only to the date when he began to write the allegory, but to the way his mind was working at the time. A case can be made out for either *The Strait Gate* (1676), or *The Heavenly Footman* which was posthumously published by Bunyan's friend Charles Doe in 1698. *The Strait Gate* is not about "the Race of Saints", but it anticipates the allegory at some points. The entrance into grace is compared to "some little pinching wicket", like the Wicket-gate which the pilgrims have to pass through; more important, the treatise concludes with some sketches of false professors closely resembling the minor type-characters of *The Pilgrim's Progress*. Formalist can be seen in "the man that hath lost all but the shell of religion", and By-Ends, the time-server, is clearly foreshadowed in the professor who

> Can be anything for any company; he can throw stones with both hands; his religion alters as fast as his company; he is a frog of Egypt, and can live in the water and out of the water. . . .[3]

But these are incidentals: mere *exempla* which Bunyan may have made use of in many sermons before he introduced them into *The Strait Gate* and into his allegory. It is *The Heavenly*

Footman which is about "the Race of Saints", for it develops
the theme of salvation under St. Paul's figure of a race for a
prize. Gradually, as if Bunyan cannot help himself, the metaphor turns from a cross-country race to a long journey. The
Christian is exhorted to "beware of by-paths", and to take
heed of the lanes that run out of the way. This recalls By-path
Meadow and other incidents in the allegory. The runner in the
race for a heavenly prize is told that he must go by the Cross,
the standing way-mark.[4] Through all the directions that are
given to him there runs the persistent general idea of striving
towards a goal across a difficult and dangerous terrain. The
grand central metaphor of *The Pilgrim's Progress* had been
conceived.

The date when *The Heavenly Footman* was written is a
matter of conjecture, but the evidence suggests it was early
rather than late. Bunyan speaks of "that little time which I have
been a professor". He recommends to his readers his own early
books, *A Few Sighs from Hell* and *The Doctrine of the Law and
Grace Unfolded* (1658–9). Finally, he employs at times a levelling
tone about the relation of masters and servants which is characteristic of his earlier phase and the revolutionary epoch in which he
had grown up. This points to a period not later than the first
imprisonment, and since *The Pilgrim's Progress* must have grown
out of the *Footman*, we are driven to the conclusion that the
former work must have been begun during Bunyan's first spell
in the county gaol. During the latter part of that time (1666–72)
there is a gap in the succession of his published tracts. Driven
in on himself, condemned by the respectable world, and
separated from his own sect, he had just produced an apologia
in the form of his spiritual autobiography. Now, in his cell, the
powerful physical imagery in which he had conceived his conversion took on a new dimension. The relation of *The Pilgrim's
Progress* to *Grace Abounding* is at a more profound level than its
relation to the *Footman*. The latter brought into the forefront
of Bunyan's mind a metaphor which countless Christian writers,
Puritans and others, had employed before. The former contains
the whole drama of the quest for personal salvation which is
the subject of the allegory. As F. M. Harrison has said: "*The
Pilgrim's Progress* is but another version of Bunyan's spiritual

autobiography, written not like that, in sombre hue, nor yet—as he claims it to be—'in black and white'—but in colours so vivid as to bring division amongst his contemporaries."[5] The good and evil presences which had haunted the depths of his consciousness were analysed psychologically in *Grace Abounding*; in the allegory they took on flesh.

The balance of evidence, then, would suggest that Bunyan began to write his *Pilgrim* after 1666 and before his release in 1672, when the break in the dream took place. In his verses he describes how some of his friends dissuaded him from printing such an experimental work. This could only be after his release, when, as their pastor, he was able fully to renew his connexion with the Bedford church. If he put the book on one side then, busy as he was with ministerial duties, it is tempting to assume that he "dreamed again" and resumed it on his second imprisonment when there was a return to the original conditions of inspiration: solitude and introspection on the militant faith for which he was suffering. This is a more likely conjecture than the assumption that he began the work during the second confinement; it would then be nearly twelve years after the appearance of *Grace Abounding*, and it would have left Bunyan very little time after his release in June or July 1677 to bring it to completion.[6]

Beyond all mere hypothesis we have this remoulding of the autobiography; psychological experience is transferred to fiction. The method of proceeding grows naturally out of the metaphorical technique of the sermon-treatise, but however much traditional lore of this kind Bunyan had absorbed, he reveals himself in the prefatory verses as a man who writes because he must: "Still as I pull'd, it came", he says, thinking of the spinner; his ideas fly "like sparks" and "breed so fast". In this upheaval of the whole man, which causes as much delight to the writer as he is about to impart, we can see the creative process at work.

II. THE THEOLOGICAL DRAMA

The First Part of *The Pilgrim's Progress* is a complete and self-sufficient narrative; it has no need of a sequel to make plain either its religious meaning or its unity of atmosphere. Considerations of literary art were not present to Bunyan's mind, except as devices for seasoning his evangelical purpose with humanity and humour, but the original version of 1678 has the unified appeal of a great poem or novel. Its note is of dramatic urgency. In the beginning of his dream the dreamer is confronted with the figure of Christian, overpowered by his consciousness of sin:

> I dreamed, and behold I saw a man cloathed with Rags, standing in a certain place, with his face from his own House, a Book in his hand, and a great burden upon his back. I looked, and saw him open the Book, and read therein; and as he read, he wept and trembled: and not being able longer to contain, he broke out with a lamentable cry; saying, what shall I do?

This vision of Christian, alone with his burden and the Bible which brings him conviction of sin, dominates the book; on to Christian Bunyan projects the terrors and soul-searchings of his own religious awakening as he described it in *Grace Abounding*; he begins at the point when he had met the godly women of Bedford, and learnt "to look into the *Bible* with new eyes", for at this period he had said in the autobiography that he was "still crying out to God, that I might know the truth, and way to Heaven and Glory". Christian's cry echoes this crying out of Bunyan, and throughout his progress towards the Promised Land the internal experience recorded in *Grace Abounding* is translated into allegorical terms, the Puritan psychology of conversion giving way stage by stage to concrete incidents and characters. The result is a book which depicts the lonely drama of the individual soul; though this is somewhat relieved in the second half of the First Part by the companionship of Hopeful (there is Faithful, too, but his martyrdom soon deprives Christian of his company). Even these friendships of Christian are friendships between individual heroes in the Christian warfare —they do not amount to any rendering of the corporate life of the church.

The Pilgrim's Progress is the book of a great convert who became able, in the tranquillity of imprisonment, not only to recollect the ardours of his conversion, but to permit their literary recrudescence into the objective, impersonal form of allegory. The modern reader who reads it after a thousand novels about "real people" must remember that the many personages whom Christian meets along the road stand for states of mind, however much Bunyan's skill at sketching in features and manners, and reproducing salty colloquial speech, has turned them into lively minor characters. Mr. Worldly Wiseman (a later addition to the First Part) talks and behaves like a well-fed respectable tradesman, but he is there to illustrate the dangerous inadequacy of a life of works without real faith. He is not a man who influences Christian, but an experience Christian undergoes. Wiseman has a jaunty self-assurance even Defoe could not have created, but we are recalled from him to the plight of Christian: Mount Sinai, representing the old law, sends out lightning and threatens to fall upon him; "Here therefore he sweat, and did quake for fear".

The outstanding scenes in this drama are combats with the powers of darkness. Each major crisis of the pilgrimage reflects some stage in Bunyan's spiritual struggles as he describes them in his autobiography. It is noteworthy that the encounter with Worldly Wiseman is a passing incident; Bunyan deals with the dangers of hypocrisy and shallow faith in some of his minor characters of observation, but the temptations which beset his central character are, like his own, those of spiritual despair. Apollyon and Giant Despair are the embodiment of the fearful voices which "plucked at" him for days together; indeed, his introspective faculty had already come near to endowing the voices with a bodily existence. Bunyan reproduces the more grotesque features of his giants and goblins from popular chap-book romance: this is Apollyon:

Now the monster was hideous to behold, he was cloathed with scales like a Fish (and they are his pride) he had Wings like a Dragon, feet like a Bear, and out of his belly came Fire and Smoke, and his mouth was as the mouth of a Lion.

But the terror of spiritual extinction symbolized by such creatures makes the conflicts with them more momentous: at a

number of points we are invited by *double-entendres* to translate
the allegory back into introspective terms: "he had almost prest
him to death, so that *Christian* began to despair of life"; "what
sighs and groans brast from *Christian's* heart" (like the groans of
the devout professor wrestling in the spirit).

The correspondence between the major incidents of the
story and the psychological crisis of a Puritan conversion invites
us to follow Bunyan's injunction, "Turn up my metaphors".
The narrative method may seem to be that of a popular
episodic romance, but there is a strong framework of Calvinist
theology underlying it. Most well-brought-up general readers
were probably able to recognize the Calvinist structure of the
book, until Evangelicalism was increasingly swamped by liberal
theology in the nineteenth century; it then became the habit
to work back from the fact of the universal appeal of *The
Pilgrim's Progress* to an erroneous picture of Bunyan as a sort of
Puritan latitudinarian. A writer in *The Gentleman's Magazine*
in 1765 reviewing *Some Account of the Imprisonment of Mr.
John Bunyan* could still regard the allegory as

> a work of imagination . . . illustrating a particular set of religious
> principles . . . it contains a most excellent epitome and illustration
> of the Calvinistic divinity under an allegory highly entertaining
> and affecting.[7]

And Coleridge saw the book as "incomparably the best *Summa
theologiae evangelicae* ever produced by a writer not miracu-
lously inspired".[8] The modern reader, remote from the tradition
of Reformed theology, and apt to think vaguely of predestination, may well expect that such a doctrine applied to a work of
fiction will deprive him of all curiosity about what is going to
happen next. We shall not do justice to Bunyan's imagination
by underestimating the importance of his theology: it is well to
grasp in outline the theological ground-plan of the allegory, and
to note the correspondences with the interior progress of *Grace
Abounding*.

The Puritans were "separated brethren" and the individual
Puritan was a man marked off from his fellows by his resolution
to treat this world as no abiding city. Thus Christian's awareness

of his state of depravity and need for grace alienates him at once from his family and the community; secular society without grace has become a city of Destruction. Then he meets Evangelist in the fields, and his conviction of sin is endorsed when the latter gives him a parchment roll on which is inscribed "Fly from the wrath to come". Only the Word of God can set the sinner on the road to salvation; Evangelist represents not so much the Word itself (the Bible) as the preaching of the Word; in his guidance of the pilgrims he is an accomplished strategist who knows how to blend gentle speech with stern admonishment when it is necessary. He suggests an idealized portrait of some great spiritual preacher, and it is natural to assume that Bunyan was here drawing John Gifford, his own guide, friend and predecessor as the minister of the Bedford congregation. The Word itself is the light which is pointed out to Christian to guide him to the Wicket-gate, and the Wicket-gate is Christ. The figure of Christ in his human nature enters little into Puritan piety. The dynamic principle in the theology of Calvin and his successors is the tension between the total depravity of fallen man and the transcendent goodness of God. To dwell much upon the Incarnation, in which divine and human are reconciled, would blur this tension; but a central place is given to Christ's sacrifice on the Cross. This is looked upon in a technical and quasi-legal fashion as a transaction in which Christ redeems the elect from sin by imputing his own righteousness to them, without any account of their individual merits. Calvin professes to find all the Fathers except Augustine unconvincing on the perplexing question of human free-will; he holds that man's will was indeed free before his fatal choice, but that after the Fall it shared in the corruption of all his other gifts; the continued use of the term "free-will" is unfortunate because of its capacity to mislead. He differs from Augustine in tracing the origin of grace to election—the marking out for salvation of a soul by God before the beginning of time—and not baptism, and in attributing the endurance of the soul in its course to the sanctifying power of grace, not to individual perseverance.[9] In *The Doctrine of the Law and Grace Unfolded* Bunyan had shown that he was completely conversant with this theology in the "covenant" form which became popular among its exponents

in the seventeenth century, and according to which God had
made a bargain with the whole number of the elect, and was
able to exploit its startling dramatic potentialities in the manner
of the enthusiastic preacher.

Christian sets off on his journey, and of two neighbours who
try to dissuade him, one, Pliable, agrees to go along with him.
When they are wallowing in the Slough of Despond, Pliable
soon pulls himself out of the mire "on that side of the Slough
which was next his own House". Christian is left to struggle in
the bog until Help shows him the steps which lead out of it
on the other side. The Slough of Despond corresponds to the
first period of Bunyan's temptation to despair; then he sometimes questioned "Whether I had any Faith or no"; and says
"I found myself on a miry bog that shook as I did but stir".

> Instead of having satisfaction, here I began to find my Soul
> to be assaulted with fresh doubts about my future happiness;
> especially with such as these, Whether I was elected? But how,
> if the Day of Grace should now be past and gone?

The steps, as the marginal note tells us, are the Promises, those
texts of the Scripture which proclaim God's mercy to the elect.
Such texts gave comfort to Bunyan in this early period of
affliction.

> One day, after I had been so many Weeks oppressed and cast
> down therewith, as I was now quite giving up the Ghost of all
> my hopes of ever attaining Life, that Sentence fell with weight
> upon my Spirit. *Look at the generations of Old and see; did ever
> any trust in God, and were confounded?* (Ecclus. ii, 10).
> . . . These words, but especially them, *And yet there is room*,
> were sweet words to me (Luke xiv, 23).

Christian now meets Worldly Wiseman and is turned aside
by him towards the town of Legality; but he is brought up
sharply by the hill that sends out lightning and threatens to fall
on his head. This represents the terrors of the Law to those
convicted of sin. Bunyan's geography is often peculiar, and this
mountain which "did hang so much over" presents no very
clear image, until we recall how in his unregenerate bell-ringing

days he was haunted by the fear that one of the bells might fall; he left off bell-ringing, but continued to watch, until the fear that the steeple itself might fall drove him away entirely.

After a chastening interview with Evangelist, Christian is set on the right road again. He arrives at the Wicket-gate which has written over it "Knock and it shall be opened unto you" (Matthew vii, 8). This is the strait gate mentioned a few verses further on in the same chapter of Matthew: ". . . strait is the gate, and narrow is the way, which leadeth unto life". This root image of the gate and the narrow path, an epitome of the whole allegory, had sunk deep into Bunyan's consciousness. The same "narrow gap, like a little doorway in the Wall" appeared in the dream he describes in *Grace Abounding*, in which he saw the elect and godly of Bedford on the sunny side of a high mountain, while he remained in frost and snow on the other side, until he was able to reach them by forcing his shoulders through the narrow passage. In Bunyan's explanation of his dream the gap, like the Wicket-gate, is Jesus Christ. Christian is admitted by Good Will; the sinner, abandoning all reliance on his own good works, throws himself on the mercy of Christ. But he has still to receive an assurance that he has been effectually called by Christ to be numbered among his elect.

The course of the pilgrimage is now interrupted by a largely static interlude, a device to be repeated later. In the Interpreter's House Christian is taken sight-seeing round a treasury of emblematic pictures. It was the duty of the Puritan convert to grow in knowledge, especially of the Bible. Soon after he began his association with the Bedford church, Bunyan made an intensive study of the Bible, right through from Genesis to Revelation, in a search for assurances against his growing doubts. Not all the pictures in the Interpreter's House are biblical, but all are supported by texts. The Interpreter may be the Holy Spirit: his ordering his servant to light the candle in order that they may see the pictures would then be a piece of that homely symbolism which appealed to Bunyan.

Refreshed by spiritual knowledge, Christian goes on his way, by a wall that is called Salvation, until he comes to the Cross. There his burden is loosed from off his shoulders and falls into the sepulchre below. Three Shining Ones appear to him; they

tell him that his sins are forgiven, give him new clothing, set a
mark on his forehead, and present him with a roll with a seal
upon it which he is to hand in at the Celestial Gate. This is the
theological hinge upon which the whole allegory turns.
Christian's sins are forgiven him by the sacrifice of Christ's
blood. "Old things are past away, all's become new": the roll is
the free pardon of Christ, the charter of Christian's election.
The incident is paralleled in *Grace Abounding*:

> Now had I an evidence, as I thought, of my Salvation from
> Heaven, with many golden Seals thereon, all hanging in my
> sight. . . .

Yet how briefly and baldly this vital episode is related in the
allegory:

> He ran thus till he came at a place somewhat ascending; and upon
> that place stood a *Cross*, and a little below in the bottom, a
> Sepulchre. So I saw in my Dream, that just as *Christian* came
> up with the *Cross*, his burden loosed from off his Shoulders . . .
> and began to tumble; and so continued to do, till it came to the
> mouth of the Sepulchre, where it fell in, and I saw it no more.
>   Then was *Christian* glad and lightsome, and said with a
> merry heart, *He hath given me Rest by his Sorrow; and Life, by
> his Death.*

Bunyan is thus brief and unemphatic because, as in his own
experience, this initiation of grace in the soul is not the end of
the drama but the beginning. The splendours and miseries of
conversion lie ahead. This episode casts a special light on the
remainder of Part One. Christian, and later Faithful and Hopeful, are fixed in the path of salvation; it is the horrors of temptation they have to undergo, not the possibility that they may
waver, which engage our attention. Later, when the pilgrims are
plunged into the worldliness of Vanity Fair, Bunyan is not
treating the temptations of the world and the flesh in their
effect on men in the manner of Spenser's Bower of Bliss, but
illustrating the persecution to be endured by the saints of God.
    Christian next passes by Simple, Sloth and Presumption,
asleep with fetters on their feet, and has a rather longer argu-

ment with Formalist and Hypocrisy. They have not come in by the Gate but have taken a short cut over the wall; that is to say, they have experienced no conversion and are not "twice-born" Christians; they rely overmuch on forms of worship. At the Hill Difficulty they will not take the hard way over the hill. They find roads which go round it and come separately to grief. Meanwhile Christian has been reduced to clambering on hands and knees to climb this emblem of spiritual struggle, and after refreshing himself in a pleasant arbour at the top he forgets his roll. Mistrust and Timorous pass him, going in the opposite direction. They speak of lions in the way, and for a moment Christian wavers; he has forgotten the promises made to him (this is the meaning of the loss of his roll) but he soon takes heart, recovers his roll, and goes on his way. The lions, when he comes to them, are chained, and are there to test the faith of pilgrims. They guard the entrace to the House Beautiful, where he is received by the porter.

Like the Interpreter's House, the House Beautiful is a place of recreation and instruction; these static episodes provide a break in the adventures along the road and recapitulate their spiritual significance. The House Beautiful symbolizes Christian's attachment to a community of believers, like Bunyan's entry into fellowship with the Bedford Separatists who had Gifford for pastor. Here he meets the damsels Discretion, Piety, Charity and Prudence; that is to say, he learns to cultivate these virtues; and here he is prepared for the battles of temptation that are to come by obtaining armour which is called All Prayer. The sisters who entertain him are gravely sympathetic and exhibit the loving simplicity of the best type of Puritan woman (Discretion "smiled, but the water stood in her eyes"). We remember the poor women of Bedford whom Bunyan found talking in the sun of the things of God.

Thus equipped, in armour of proof from the armoury where he had seen curiously exhibited "the Jaw bone with which Samson did such mighty feats" and other marvels, Christian descends into the Valley of Humiliation. This valley and its neighbour, the Valley of the Shadow of Death, provide the strongest spiritual terrors of his pilgrimage, apart from the imprisonment in Doubting Castle. In the first valley Christian

F

meets the foul fiend Apollyon, who asks him to transfer his
allegiance from God to Satan, who is his original master;
the idea is that of feudal allegiance to a lord, with the claim of a
rival lord on the vassal's services. This leads to a pitched
battle of the St. George and the Dragon type, emotionally
in keeping with the characterization of Christian as a loyal
knight. In the background is the text: "No man can serve
two masters." Bunyan is giving palpable form to the period of
temptation described in *Grace Abounding* as "a very great
storm", when he too was tormented by the urge to give his
allegiance completely to the evil powers:

> Sometimes, also, he would cast in such wicked thoughts as these:
> that I must pray to him or for him. I have thought sometimes
> of that—*Fall down*, or *if thou wilt fall down and worship me.*

For his description of the Valley of the Shadow of Death,
Bunyan draws on his memory of the worst hallucinations
which oppressed him at this time. The devil who whispers
many grievous blasphemies into his ear, the sensation of being
pursued, the general darkness, recalling his reiterated statement
that in these moods of despair all sensible things became disgusting to him—all are present. But at this moment of horror,
the impregnability of Christian's faith is emphasized by a fine
stroke of drama:

> When *Christian* had travelled in this disconsolate condition
> some considerable time, he thought he heard the voice of a
> man, as going before him, saying, *Though I walk through the
> valley of the shadow of death, I will fear none ill, for thou art with
> me.*

This is the voice of Faithful, whom Christian does not come up
with till the light of the following day. His utter loneliness is to
be relieved by a companion; but this companion is another
lonely hero, fighting his own fight, who "knew not what to
answer, for that he also thought himself to be alone".

The daylight comes: in terms of the allegory of the soul,
again the promises are remembered and the mists of doubt dis-
persed; "His candle shineth in my head, and by his light I go

through darkness" (Job xxix, 3). Christian emerges from the valley, passing by the cave of Giants Pope and Pagan, who are too feeble to trouble him; the former, "by reason of age, and also of the many shrewd brushes he met with in his younger days", has "grown crazy and stiff in his joints". The meeting with Faithful takes place, and the two pilgrims compare travel notes as they journey on together. This is an exchange of experience such as might take place between Puritan converts, and it forms another interlude of recapitulation, for Faithful's progress is naturally parallel to that of Christian, with minor variations in the symbolism: the Old Man of St. Paul ("Put off the old man") is introduced as a personification of original sin; he gives Faithful "a deadly twitch back", when he tries to escape from his blandishments, and Faithful, because he has wavered, incurs a severe drubbing from Moses (the power of the old law) until Christ comes to his aid. The episode is prolonged by their encounter with Talkative, the glib, showy professor, who can discuss all the commonplaces of twice-born religion, "but he knows but only to *talk* of them". This conversation is most important for our understanding of the theology of *The Pilgrim's Progress*. Faithful is more inclined to dialectic than Christian, and he makes a number of things clear which might otherwise cause difficulty. So far the symbolism has been concerned entirely with the acceptance of certain dogmas and the recognition of grace in the soul; do all the strivings of the pilgrimage belong solely to the inner life, and how do Christian and Faithful stand in regard to the ordinary moral world of everyday behaviour? Faithful points the contrast with Talkative's mechanical complacency: "Saying and Doing are two things", and "the Soul of Religion is the practick part". Grace only discovers itself by a hunger after righteousness. As the marginal note says, "True knowledge attended with endeavours." Thus religious hypocrisy is dealt with, a dangerous vice for Puritans.

Evangelist now visits the pilgrims again, congratulates them on their progress so far, and exhorts them to be prepared for the martyrdom of one or both of them in the town of Vanity. They enter Vanity Fair. There is realistic satire here on the way of the world; the crowded market with its "*Britain* Row, *French* Row,

Italian Row", and so on, inspired, among other artists, George Cruikshank. But behind the satirical humour lies an intense vision of the World in the theological sense and the Christian's separation from it. So uncompromising is this vision that in the catalogue of the merchandise at the fair "Whores, Bawds, Wives, Husbands, Children, Masters, Servants", are enumerated together without discrimination. Christian and Faithful soon call attention to themselves by their singularity and their desire to buy nothing but truth; they are exposed in a cage, imprisoned, and finally brought to trial before a packed jury containing Mr. Blind-mind, Mr. Malice, Mr. Love-lust and Mr. Implacable. Bunyan is shifting the allegory from the saga of conversion to the plight of the gospel Christian in the contemporary world; he is recalling his own arrest, his examination before the justices and his subsequent trial and imprisonment. The trial scene, shot through by personal experience, was to be worked over by Bunyan again in *The Holy War*. Faithful is condemned to death, but Christian is remanded back to prison. From there he makes his escape with a new friend, Hopeful, who has been converted by the behaviour of Christian and Faithful at the Fair. The episode shows that the proper climax of the Christian life may be martyrdom; the distribution of the ideal Christian between two characters makes it possible to illustrate at the same time the normal progress of the believer towards a natural death-bed; and Bunyan's own projection of himself into his vision contains both the internal man, "saved by grace", and the tinker-martyr of Bedford county gaol, a hero of the church.

There intervenes, as usual after one of the high actions of the drama, a passage of edifying conversation. The pilgrims meet By-Ends, who comes from the town of Fair-speech. While Talkative was a Holy Willie, By-Ends is a temporizing Vicar of Bray who is "always most zealous when Religion goes in his Silver Slippers", and Christian and Hopeful make short work of him. The whole episode was added in the third edition; it lies apart from the main allegory of the soul, and shows how Bunyan's interest turned more and more to humorous satire.

Passing now across a pleasant plain called Ease, Christian and Hopeful come to where Demas guards a silver mine a little off the highway; many pilgrims have perished on the treacherous ground by it, for it is Hill Lucre. Demas is chosen as the symbol of covetousness because of St. Paul's words about him ("Demas hath forsaken me, having loved this present world", 2 Timothy, iv, 10). Christian and Hopeful pass by, but By-Ends and his companions fall an easy prey to him. The pilgrims learn precepts of caution from the pillar of salt into which Lot's wife was changed. Another idyllic landscape unfolds itself before them, rich in associations from the Psalms and Isaiah, and in the deep spiritual suggestiveness which Bunyan can always impart to fresh green meadows and clear water. The pilgrims rest by the River of the Water of Life. All seems to be going well for them; but it is in moments of ease like this that the tempter springs upon the professor and torments him with fresh doubts about his election. They stray into By-Path Meadow and are soon in the dungeon of Doubting Castle, the prisoners of Giant Despair.

The brisk fairy-tale narration must not make us forget that this episode is a study of spiritual malaise, like the Slough of Despond and the struggle with Apollyon. In this giant with his crabtree cudgel, theology may seem to have given place to pure chap-book adventure, the raw-head-and-bloody-bones of some black-letter *Seven Champions of Christendom* found on the stalls of Stourbridge Fair. Chance and danger may appear to have reasserted themselves in a world freed from the compulsion of Calvinist determinism. But this is not so, for during all their perils Christian carries with him the means of their deliverance:

> Now a little before it was day, good *Christian*, as one half amazed, brake out in this passionate Speech, *What a fool*, quoth he, *am I thus to lie in a stinking Dungeon, when I may as well walk at liberty! I have a Key in my bosom, called* Promise, *that will, I am persuaded, open any Lock in* Doubting Castle. Then said *Hopeful*, That's good news; good Brother, pluck it out of thy bosom and try.

God's covenant with his elect has not been forgotten; Christian can only neglect it for a time, till his own regenerate heart recalls him to the promise of faith. No allegorical intermediary brings him the key; it is with him all the time, emphasizing at the expense of narrative plausibility a principle of Puritan psychology. Escape is now certain, though the story-teller in Bunyan makes the iron outer gate of the castle difficult to force: "but that lock went damnable hard". Sir Charles Firth, and Professor Talon after him, have seen in this Bunyan's colloquial warmth getting the better of the proprieties.[10] There is also a grim theological pun involving the whole conception of the soul's struggle against the despair which means damnation.

The episode, like others, has its parallel in the inner pilgrimage of *Grace Abounding*. It recalls the time when he feared he had betrayed Christ like Judas and committed the sin against the Holy Ghost. He was ceaselessly haunted by a terrible text: "For ye know how that afterward, when he would have inherited the blessing, he was rejected: for he found no place of repentance, though he sought it carefully, with tears" (Hebrews xii, 17). It seems in Bunyan's later analysis of this temptation (§§ 236–52) that, unlike his other trials, this one was caused by a misunderstanding which played into Satan's hands, not by a direct attack from the powers of darkness. The chief point is that he was deluded: he never surrendered Christ voluntarily, but his spiritual inexperience made him believe that he had. He had not fully understood the promises. All the metaphors of Doubting Castle are present in this analysis:

> Now did my Chains fall off my legs indeed; I was loosed from my Affliction and irons; my Temptations also fled away. . . .
> The Scriptures now also were wonderful things unto me. I saw that the truth and verity of them were the Keys of the Kingdom of Heaven.

Most of the dangers are now past and the end is in sight. In Immanuel's Land, another delightful pastoral landscape, Christian and Hopeful lean on their staves talking to the shepherds: it is an archetypal picture of the wayfaring man of all ages. From the hill called Clear they have a glimpse of the celestial city through the shepherds' perspective glass. The remaining adventures are theologically vague, and, as adventures, somewhat tame. There is a long dialectical interlude with the "brisk lad" Ignorance, the excellently told anecdote of Little-faith, the pilgrims' encounter with a black man who is the Flatterer, and who leads them astray, and their chastisement by an angel. They meet Atheist, and grow sleepy in crossing the Enchanted Ground, until Hopeful gives an account of his spiritual experience. This is the last time they are to exchange godly arguments, dividing their discourse into numbered heads like a sermon, for now they enter the land of Beulah. Bunyan now turns from the translation of his spiritual states into allegory to a rapt evocation of the traditional Christian paradise. From being colloquial, the language becomes reminiscent of the poetry of Canticles, Isaiah and Revelation: "as the Bridegroom rejoyceth over the Bride, so did their God rejoyce over them". The terror of death to weak human nature is not glossed over: Christian and Hopeful are "much stounded" at the river they must cross. Christian begins to sink in the water, and all his worse fears and hallucinations return to press upon him, but his companion bears him up. The Puritan pilgrim's life is a struggle to the very end. At last they are across the river, and are received with music and white raiment in the heavenly city. Had Bunyan been a religious artist according to the modern notion, which sees formal literary perfection as somehow analogous to spiritual achievement, he would have ended his work here amid the paeans of the saints. But his evangelical purpose was paramount and overrode any such decorum. Anxiety had dogged Christian throughout his pilgrimage, and to show that this anxiety had objective justification, though it was ultimately groundless in Christian's case, he ends by showing us where the brisk lad Ignorance is led by his sense of false security. He knocks at the gate but cannot produce his "Certificate", and the same two angels who have conducted Christian and Hopeful to the City bind him hand and foot and take him away. "Then I saw that there was a way to Hell, even from the Gates of Heaven, as from the City of *Destruction*." The dreamer awakes.

Christian and Hopeful, then, had their certificates, while Ignorance had not. This might seem to confirm the view that for the ordinary reader Calvinism drains away all dramatic interest from the Christian life in the world, leaving the Field of Folk as the scene of an uneventful march to the scaffold or the throne.

How can a progress of which the end is fore-ordained keep the interest of a novel? Yet the attraction of the work does not lie primarily in its romantic variety of incident, nor do the vigour and purity of the English explain the whole of its appeal. Christian's agonized striving holds our attention because we look through his eyes and share his own uncertainty about the outcome, even though on a longer view of divine purpose there is no uncertainty. It has been remarked that the two great sins of Puritanism were excess of confidence leading to hypocrisy, and diffidence leading to despair of vocation.[11] The latter was often the more grievous. But since the days of the spiritual brethren it had been maintained by the preachers that the elect were specially liable to such doubts. We find, for instance, in John Dod:

> Those that have obtained the pardon of sinne, doe of all others most desier further assurance of itt, as David ps. 51.
> Reasons:
> 1. Because they have tasted the sweetnes of Christes righteousnes.
> 2. They feele the want of faith, and the bitterness of sinne and unbeleef.
> 3. Because Sathan drives them off to doubting.
> 4. Their sanctification is imperfect, and ther are daily breaches made into godes image. . . .
> He that doubtes not of the maine point, may for all that be full of heavines in want of feeling, as a sonn, that is sure to be his fathers heir comming to his howse in a stormy night. If the dores showld be shutt against him, and a mastive turned loose uppon him, woulld itt not dismay him?[12]

Richard Sibbes preached a series of sermons specially for such doubting Christians, and said:

> Some againe are haunted with hideous representations to their fantasies, and with vile and unworthy thoughts of God, of CHRIST, of the Word, &C. which as busie flies disquiet and molest their peace. . . . A pious soule is no more guilty of them, than *Benjamin* of *Josephs* cup put into his sack.[13]

and elsewhere he writes:

Thus we see that the life of a Christian is trouble upon trouble, as wave upon wave. God will not suffer us to rest in security, but one way or other he will fire us out of our starting holes, and make us to run after him; how much better were it for us then ... *to run as we may obtaine.* ...[14]

III. THE CHARACTERS

One literary consequence of Bunyan's theology is that there is no possibility of a treatment of the full life of man like that in Catholic allegory, or even in Spenser. The power of final perseverance granted to the pilgrims in election limits the range of human experience Bunyan can deal with. Thus the Hill Lucre episode does not treat avarice with anything like the fullness of Spenser's picture of the Cave of Mammon: Guyon is led aside from the way; he falls to rise again. A few words shouted from the roadside are all that Christian needs to settle with Demas: there is no question of a choice of two ways of life presented and a decision to be made. Christian has "heard of this place before now"; it is By-Ends and his companions who go over "at the first beck", and perish in the pit. Likewise Faithful's encounter with Wanton is the merest flirtation with the sins of the flesh. It is only in Part Two that we get something of the rich bustle of the life of believers in society. But that was written years later in the time of Bunyan's fame and prosperity: its atmosphere is altogether more mellow. In Part One the humorous passages are mostly about backsliders and heretics. Yet Bunyan's world, so conscientiously symbolic in each detail, everywhere retains the savour of common life. It is in these character sketches that his genius for realistic observation is exercised in a manner which prevents the conversion allegory from becoming too inward and obsessed. The source from which Bunyan drew for his main characters— Christian, Faithful and Hopeful—was his own introspective imagination. However, in his pictures of the reprobate and in his account of the ups and downs of the way we see his sharp eye for behaviour and his sardonic humour. There is no real division in his imagination between this gift of observation and his

introspective faculty; both are strongly visual: it is the same
quality of mind which conveys types of character by fixing on
small traits of gesture, and which reduces Scripture texts to
concrete, touchable presences.

Before we come to this gallery of minor characters there is
the King's Highway itself to be taken into account. Bunyan has
rendered his great primary metaphor of the Christian's journey
through life in terms of a seventeenth-century journey. His
highway is an English highway such as Celia Fiennes might have
travelled on, with its miry slough at one point and "a fine
pleasant green lane" running into it at another. The Slough of
Despond may have only a little exaggerated the dangers of
such roads under flood water: we hear of one of Bunyan's flock
fearing to venture, "the wayes being soe dirty and deepe". Then
there was the danger from footpads: the story of Little-faith
gives a graphic, naturalistic account of highway robbery:

> Now there happened, at that time, to come down that *Lane* from
> *Broad-way-gate* three sturdy Rogues, and their names were
> *Faint-heart*, *Mistrust* and *Guilt*. . . . So they all came up to him,
> and with threatening language bid him *stand*. At this, *Little
> faith* lookt as white as a Clout, and had neither power to fight nor
> fly.

Here the transformation of theology (the perpetual subject of
doubt about assurance) into realistic incident bids fair to
banish the former into a corner of the mind.

But there are limits to the realism of background. When the
story requires landscape different from the flat Bedfordshire
sort, Bunyan, who knew no other, is apt to be extraordinarily
vague. Hypocrisy stumbles and falls in "a wide field full of dark
mountains". Again, the Delectable Mountains, and those landscapes which give a foretaste of the Promised Land, possess
"Vineyards, and Fountains of water", and the pilgrims "see
every day the flowers appear in the earth, and hear the voice
of the Turtle in the Land". This is not Bedfordshire, but the
Palestine of the Old Testament. On the other hand, Vanity
Fair, with its rows of stalls, "as in other fairs of less moment",
Britain Row, Italian Row, and so on, reminds us of a real

country fair as much as it points the scriptural text about vanity. Bunyan must have seen the great fair held at Stourbridge, which had its own court to try offences committed within its precincts. Vanity Fair has its court, and the proceedings in it introduce yet another realistic overtone into the allegory: here we have informers, a judge who abuses the prisoners, and a packed jury; drawing partly on his own experiences, and partly on what he had heard of treason trials, Bunyan is indicating what sort of justice Dissenters might expect in the age of Judge Jeffreys.

As Christian and his companions travel along this highway which has so many of the characteristics of a seventeenth-century provincial road, they meet some dubious persons whose credentials as pilgrims are suspect. Bunyan's literary art is displayed in its full subtlety in these portraits: they are portraits of heretics and backsliders, and the art is that of a popular preacher intent only on making his exposure of the reprobates humorously convincing. The result is a group of moral types which have been given all the liveliness of individuals by a deft etching in of a few dominant features and gestures. The features are symbolic, but the symbol always carries a humorous, realistic outside. By-Ends's great-grandfather was "a Waterman, looking one way, and rowing another". Talkative is "a tall man, and something more comely at a distance than at hand". Ignorance is "a very brisk lad". This last trait is hardly symbolic at all, and as description of a type is very slight, yet it somehow hits off the glib superficiality of the character better than a more elaborate analysis. Mr. Worldly Wiseman is "a Gentleman", and his conversational tone towards Christian has a patronizing bluster which befits his assumption of social superiority:

How now, good fellow, whither away after this burdened manner? . . .
Hast thou a Wife and Children?

In fact, all these characters have a double mode of operation: in the strict terms of the allegory they are heresies personified (Ignorance, not Ignorant), but at the same time they present the likeness of individual heretics. The method is that of the traditional sermon-example; in the popular religious literature of the middle ages there are character sketches comparable to those of Bunyan in their economical construction and blend of doctrine and dramatic reality. There is the angry man of the *Ancren Riwle*, puffing out his cheeks like a trumpeter, and Langland's Covetousness, who was "beetle-browed and blubber-lipped, and his cheeks hung slackly like a leather purse".

It is noteworthy that almost all the sins exposed are those incident to a gathered congregation. Bunyan is writing, as he preached, for godly people of his own persuasion; he probably never expected that his work would find approval far beyond the frontiers of Baptist and Independent orthodoxy, any more than he can have foreseen how it would transcend social barriers. Thus there are only the most cursory encounters with people in the outer darkness, like Atheist, and even the simpler varieties of false profession, in the persons of Formalist and Hypocrisy, are not treated at length. Hypocrisy is a complex sin for Puritans, their great weakness in their dealings with others, as spiritual diffidence was their principal interior enemy. Bunyan needs three characters to illustrate three chief branches of it. Talkative is the man who possesses all the right ideas and has converted them to formulas and jargon. He can talk of the new birth and the necessity of a work of grace in the soul, but he has not the root of the matter in him. By-Ends is less self-deceived; he has an eye to the main chance, and it is not surprising to find that his friends are Mr. Hold-the-World, Mr. Money-love, and Mr. Save-all (the latter represents the error of those who believe in universal salvation). He is shifty and never makes a really plain statement; he will not even tell the pilgrims his name. With his companions he indulges in a parody of the kind of profitable discourse held by Christian and Hopeful, in order to decide how a minister may square his conscience when aiming at a rich benefice. Ignorance provides a puzzle. His speech may be irritatingly complacent, but it does not communicate a stale odour of moral corruption, like By-Ends's; on the surface he seems an ingenuous youth, and James Foster, an enlightened eighteenth-century Dissenting preacher, used to say that none of the characters in *The Pilgrim's Progress* spoke sense except Ignorance. His damnation at the end comes as a shock to the modern reader's idea of moral, as well as literary, propriety. The point about him is that he is wilfully ignorant; in spite of the entreaties of Christian, he persists in the greatest intellectual error imaginable to a Calvinist: he relies on his own righteousness ("a good heart and a good life according to God's commandments") and rejects the free grace of Christ. Such persistence would seem to a Puritan clear evidence of reprobation. Christian's stern beliefs seem to him "whimsies . . . the fruit of distracted brains". This is the cool, sceptical language of a man of the new age, a man of latitude, anxious to ground his faith in conscience and conduct, not in twice-born experience. Bunyan had emerged from a bitter controversy with the latitudinarian Edward Fowler; memories of that feud may have contributed to the harsh treatment bestowed on the "brisk lad".[15]

The *Church Book* would suggest that Bunyan was able to study many of his moral types among the delinquent members of Bedford Meeting, a broadly inclusive body. In all the people of the pilgrimage we see Bunyan's novel handling of the very ancient tradition of allegory, which was now falling into disrepute. In relation to the great flowering of that tradition in *Piers Plowman*, or even in as late a work as *The Faerie Queene*, *The Pilgrim's Progress* is a crude popular survival, devoid of the imaginative complexity of the old allegoric mood. Piers the Plowman carries a number of meanings, the ideal labourer, the life of Christ, the work of the Church, and so on; in medieval allegory, abstract moral qualities and ideas are embodied and there are different levels of suggestiveness in these embodiments. Bunyan sees only one thing at a time, or rather, in order to visualize a moral quality he has to circumscribe it within the narrow but powerful outline of a type. But if Bunyan is the end of an old song, he is also the beginning of a new one. His allegory has a concrete strength which the old allegory never had, and his moral types could provide minor characters for a Restoration play or an eighteenth-century novel; his simplicity is only partly naïve, and partly the naked, just observation of a new order of feeling. Even the heroic figure of Christian, with his cry of "Life, life, eternal life", who holds together these particulars of observation, can appear later in a "character-part" as the seasoned spiritual campaigner who "snibbeth his fellow", the young Hopeful, and puts him in his place. For, after all, Christian himself is a transcript from life: the physician of souls with a shrewd eye for back-sliders had faithfully observed his own spiritual growth.

IV. THE TRADITIONAL MATERIAL: SACRED AND PROFANE

Like many great books *The Pilgrim's Progress* is at the same time both daringly original and deeply rooted in tradition. Bunyan used the conceptions of Puritan psychology to interpret a genuine religious experience; to give literary expression to his vision of the Christian life he had recourse to a metaphor much older than Puritanism, which goes back to Christ's words to the apostles exhorting them to take nothing for their journey (Luke ix, 6). It is one of those archetypal images which are larger than metaphors because the idea seems to appeal to a deep and universal feeling about human life as a progressive development from birth to death; the term of comparison is felt to be, not an embroidery on the facts, but nearer to ultimate reality than the experience described. Throughout the Christian centuries the image was perpetuated by preaching tradition, and by literary allegories like Langland's *Piers Plowman*, and its influence was reinforced and given a more precise form by the actual custom of pilgrimage in the middle ages.[16]

In Victorian times, when Bunyan, like Robert Burns, was acclaimed as a child of nature, it was thought necessary to defend him from a possible charge of plagiarism on the ground that his work had been preceded by so many closely analogous pilgrimage allegories. George Offor conscientiously examined scores of books for this purpose. Bunyan had no need to look at books for an idea which was so widely diffused and which had entered into the blood stream of Christendom. There were charges of plagiarism in his own day, and he indignantly rebutted them in the verses prefixed to *The Holy War*:

Some say *The Pilgrim's Progress* is not mine.

He was guiltless just because his debt to generations of Christian consciousness was so deep; but he owed also a special debt to the literary forms evolved by the Puritans since the spiritual brethren of Elizabeth's reign, and he paid it amply by fusing three different types of popular religious discourse into an organic narrative whole. His transformation of the spiritual autobiography has already been discussed. He also makes use of two other forms: first, the popular sermon or treatise which concentrated upon the "uses", or practical applications, of doctrine, and employed a vigorous plain style and a wealth of homely imagery; next, the expository dialogue, in which speakers representing various stock types of Christian and non-believer discuss points of theology and moral conduct.

In regard to the figurative sermon, it may be said that Bunyan inherited that literary form at the highest stage of its development. The plain style prescribed by the Spirit did not forbid any stratagem which might win souls. So "Similitudes and Comparisons" flourished, to be indicated in the margin by a sign manual, as a mark of their popularity, when the sermons were published. The two great stock metaphors of the Christian life, as a pilgrimage, and as a war to the death against a ruthless foe, both abounded in Puritan sermons and lectures before the Civil War; both answered to the real condition of the Puritan minority between the age of Cartwright and the Act of Toleration. Often the sermon becomes a harmony of moral lessons and subsidiary comparisons based on one of these themes, or some other single image. John Downame's monumental *The Christian Warfare* makes the military image the controlling principle of an evangelical handbook. Thomas Adams, "the Shakespeare of the Puritans", develops a series of variations on the pilgrimage theme in his sermon *The Christian's Walk: or, The King's Highway of Charity*:

As clear, near, and sociable a way as love is, yet few can hit it; for of all ways you shall find this least travelled. Others know there is such a way, but they will not set their foot into it. Their old way of malice and covetousness is delightful . . . the entrance to this way is somewhat sharp and unpleasant to flesh; for it begins at repentance for former uncharitableness.[17]

Meanwhile most of Bunyan's minor Biblical images had been anticipated in sermon treatment. Thomas Adams hits upon the very words Bunyan chose later in *The Strait Gate* and in the allegory, when he describes the entrance into the society of the saints by the narrow door of sanctification: "A city beautiful and roomy; yet it hath but a narrow wicket, a little gate;"[18] Thomas Goodwin, preaching on anxiety about election, speaks of the name of Christ as a staff in the valley of the shadow of death;[19] and Thomas Taylor discusses sin as a burden that presses down upon man like an actual load.[20] William Perkins and Richard Bernard, the chief theorists of Puritan rhetoric, had formally justified the preacher's use of similitudes, provided that, like those in the Scriptures, they were drawn from things known, apt, and easy to be conceived.[21]

In sermons with linked similitudes the movement from homily to symbolic narrative had already begun before the Civil War. The decisive change which lifts *The Pilgrim's Progress* into another category comes when the sermon containing popular "applications" is, as it were, turned inside out: the homely comparisons become the main stream of the narrative, and the Biblical references and moral comment are consigned to the margin, or to the interspersed tags of verse. A more daring attempt to transform the sermon into an edifying fiction in this manner is found even before Bunyan in Richard Bernard's *The Isle of Man*.[22] Bunyan probably knew Bernard's book, which makes effective play with legal procedure, and there are parallels between the realistic trial of the vices in Bernard and the great trial scene in *The Holy War*. But *The Isle of Man* is one of those works which depend on a good, if not very subtle, idea, rather than any special merits of execution. It is interesting to notice that Bernard, like Bunyan after him, felt that such an excursion into fiction needed a special explanation. He adds an apology which employs the same arguments as those used in Bunyan's prefatory verses, particular stress being laid on Christ's example in his parables. Both Bunyan and Bernard are afraid lest their allegory be too daringly humorous ("Put thee into a laughter or a feud") and compromise with the unregenerate while giving offence to the pious.

The modern reader ignores the extent of this humour, and the broad and incongruous effects it can produce (like Matthew's gripe-mixture in Part Two) because he does not read homilies at all for ordinary purposes of instruction, and can only approach the religious message through the literary effect. Devotional books were the everyday literary food of the seventeenth century, and *The Pilgrim's Progress* appeared extraordinarily lively and different because, in a multitude of sober treatises, the homilist had never gone quite so far. Yet the simile was there, and theory was there to justify it. Many had reached the point Bunyan reached in *The Heavenly Footman* when he found himself slipping unawares into an allegory, and had resisted the impulse; resistance was easier, since few had a store of inner experience such as Bunyan had, to give vitality to their fiction, or could choose a dream, not as a conventional vehicle, but as the natural expression of the unconscious mind.

Another branch of homiletic tradition, the expository dialogue, provides the source for the static episodes of edifying conversation between pilgrims and heretics which break up the story into sections. The most outstanding example of this genre was Arthur Dent's *The Plaine Mans Path-way to Heaven* (1601), which was one of the two books Bunyan's first wife brought him as her marriage portion. Dent's claim that it is "written dialogue-wise for the better understanding of the simple" emphasizes the evangelical purpose to which all Puritan literary techniques were subordinated; and his book is better worth remembering on this account, as a landmark in the continuity of colloquial prose for religious ends; but the dialogue form clearly influenced Bunyan in these conversations and later in *Mr. Badman*. In Dent's work, Theologus, who is like the Wiseman of *Badman*, instructs Philagathus (the honest man) and Asunetos (the ignorant man) and resists the cavillings of Antilegon (the Atheist). It is very much like the debate with Ignorance: there is the same curious combination of racy speech with abstract argument, the same total absence of character-development or progress in the story. The fiction is the merest skeleton, a dialectical progress towards the inevitable final conviction of Asunetos. But a background

of real life is suggested, and this is what constitutes the
importance of Dent's work. *The Life and Death of Mr. Badman*
would have been impossible without Dent, and by judiciously
blending his manner with a freer use of narrative, Bunyan
was able to include more doctrine than could have been con-
veyed in a faster-moving story. Hopeful's very important
recapitulation of the stages of his conversion is an excursus
of this type.

In the more stirring portions of the narrative, the battles
with giants and monsters, Bunyan recalls the marvels of the
chap-book romances which had delighted his profane youth;
he had looked back on those graceless days in *A Few Sighs
from Hell* (1658):

> Alas! What is the Scripture? Give me a ballad, a news-book,
> George on horseback, or Bevis of Southampton; give me some
> book that teaches curious arts, that tells of old fables; but for the
> holy Scriptures I cared not.[23]

"George on horseback" is the folk-hero St. George. Bunyan
probably knew Richard Johnson's *The Seven Champions of
Christendom* (1597), a debased popular version of chivalrous
romance which went through many black-letter editions in the
seventeenth century. St. George, when wounded in the fight
with the dragon, is healed by the leaves of a miraculous tree:
in Christian's combat with Apollyon, the hero is restored by
leaves from the tree of life. The giant Blanderon, like Giant
Maul in Part Two, wields an enormous club. The mysterious
episode of the Enchanted Ground where the pilgrims fall asleep
may owe something to the garden of the magician Ormandine
where St. David falls under a spell: "All his senses were over-
taken with a sudden and heavy sleep"; and the arming of the
hero by ladies in the House Beautiful finds an echo in every
romance worth its salt.

Bunyan absorbed this romantic lore into his youthful
mind, as he absorbed all the other influences of seventeenth-
century popular culture. He was the child of Stourbridge Fair,
before he became the convert of Geneva and Amsterdam. But
though provincial England nurtured his art, his religious
experience brought it to birth; his gatherings from these idle

tales were driven deep down into his being during the period of terror and remorse which initiated his conversion; in prison, during the recrudescence of experience which preceded creation, ideas from romance and from the Bible became blended into an imaginative harmony. It would be utterly wrong to conceive of the Puritanism as a thin crust spread upon the romantic appetite of the folk for giants and marvels. In his attitude to the Bible, Bunyan is like a child or a man of little reading not far from childhood, who interprets a poem or a story by an old illustration which fills his mind and excludes fresh impressions. Thus in the Valley of the Shadow of Death, he sees the inner spiritual world of the Psalms in terms of popular romance: hobgoblins walk it, and it is strewn with the bones of former adventurers. Again, the martyrdom of Faithful, in its fantastic barbarity, seems to be based on a vivid pictorial recollection of the fearsome woodcuts in Foxe's *Acts and Monuments*.

One less important influence may be noticed. Again, it is more pictorial than literary. When the Interpreter takes Christian into his significant rooms he shows him a series of emblem pictures. The emblem is a symbolic picture, usually accompanied by a sententious motto and an explanatory poem. Emblem books enjoyed an immense vogue in most European countries during the sixteenth and seventeenth centuries; secular emblems were succeeded by sacred ones, and the emblem collections of Quarles and Wither reached a wide Puritan public. The form had begun as a courtly amusement, in a pre-scientific age when the visible world was seen as the harmonious expression of spiritual qualities; the material was everywhere informed by spirit, and the most ordinary things had a moral lesson to teach. The scientific revolution of the seventeenth century, which separated mind from matter, shook the prestige of the allegory and the emblem; emblems became a diversion for the vulgar. Bunyan's use of them reminds us how much of his mental world antedates Cartesianism and the Royal Society. Late in life he composed his own emblem book, *A Book for Boys and Girls*: in his hands the form has become a vehicle for teaching piety to children, and to any grown-ups who may be charmed by so prettily gilded a pill.[24]

Many of the Interpreter's emblems can be traced to earlier collections, especially those of Quarles and Wither. In one of them, a typical example, a man tries to sweep a dusty room, but it only makes the dust rise, until a damsel sprinkles water; then it can be cleaned "with Pleasure". The dusty room is the unregenerate heart; the broom is the Law, and the water is the new law of the Gospel. There is an emblem like this by Wiericx, the Dutch emblematist, and it may have reached Bunyan from some intermediate source, perhaps a sermon "similitude". Even Bunyan's main metaphor had been anticipated in earlier emblem pictures: Geffrey Whitney, the Elizabethan emblematist, has an illustration which shows a pilgrim equipped with scrip and staff turning his back on a geographical globe of the world, and setting his face towards the rising sun. In the margin are the words *Peregrinus Christianus loquitur*.[25] But, as we have already noticed, the pilgrim metaphor was widely diffused in the seventeenth century, and both George Herbert and the Puritan poet Quarles wrote poems on this theme which translate the emblem technique into verse.

The Jesuit devotional books of the Counter-Reformation bequeathed their emotional and baroque imagery to the emblem tradition. The fire of grace at work in the human heart and the oil of God which nourishes it belong to this genre; however, the temper of Bunyan's mind, so far removed from the rapturous or the exotic, has bent this foreign material into a plain and everyday pattern by a few deft touches. The devil is symbolized by a man on the other side of the wall casting water on the fire: the presence of this wall and a man with a bucket of water reduces the mystical flame to an ordinary farmyard bonfire.

Bunyan's resort to emblems has an importance beyond the quaint details of the Interpreter's House. It shows how much he still retained of the old spiritualized world-picture, in spite of his forward-looking attempt to express morality in terms of character. In *Solomon's Temple Spiritualized* (1688) he says:

Since it is the wisdom of God to speak to us ofttimes by trees, gold, silver, stones, beasts, fowls, fishes, spiders, ants, frogs,

flies, lice, dust, &c., and here by wood; how should we by them
understand his voice, if we count there is no meaning in them?[26]

v. The Style: Biblical and Colloquial

It is of course impossible to imagine *The Pilgrim's Progress*
without the English Bible. In Bunyan, Puritan bibliolatry
found its poet. But the general staple of his diction and rhythm
is popular and colloquial, not biblical. The natural tendency
to salute Bunyan as a man of one book was already at work in
his lifetime. The friend who wrote the anonymous *Life and
Works of Mr. John Bunyan* describes the slender collection of
books he had with him in prison:

There also I surveyed his library; the least and yet the best that
ever I saw.[27]

But the supremacy of the Bible over Puritan Englishmen
meant that it was endlessly preached and commented on.
Bunyan was a great preacher who worked over and published
his sermons. Together with the tradition of similitudes which he
inherited from the spiritual brethren, he was heir to the racy,
vigorous manner of the popular preacher. His language is
simple in an elemental sense: it is entirely his own, for he
writes as he must have spoken, except in great set passages
like the crossing of the pilgrims over the river of death, where
the rhythms are more conscious. His language often has a
kind of brutal roughness, sometimes a crude humour, and
always he has at his command proverbs and illustrations, the
untraceable and unclassifiable prudential lore of the countryside.
Christian "snibbeth" Hopeful for expressing an unadvised
theological opinion, and says, "Thou speakest as one upon whose
Head the shell is still to this day." "Every Fatt (i.e. vessel)
must stand upon his own bottom," says Presumption. Mrs.
Lightmind relates her visit to Madam Wanton; "where we
were as merry as the maids". Provincial forms occur like the
frequentative "scrabble" (Little-faith, after his highway robbery,
"made a shift to scrabble on his way"); and unstressed spoken

forms, as when Timorous, in Part Two, "would a had him gone back for fear of the Lyons". Bunyan employs this fund of common speech with a natural eloquence that is all his own; he creates his own proverbial sentences, as when Christian says of Talkative:

> His house is as empty of Religion, *as the white of an Egg is of savour*.

When the occasion calls for it, he can exchange the short, broken phrases of conversation for longer rhythmical units, in which emphatic monosyllabic words are so distributed as to create a more musical pattern. This is well demonstrated in the opening words:

> As I walk'd through the wilderness of this world, I lighted on a certain place, where was a Den; and I laid me down in that place to sleep: and as I slept I dreamed a Dream.

The disposition of "world . . . Den . . . sleep . . . Dream" reveals the unconscious art which lifts Bunyan above the multitude of good, natural writers produced by that age; simple, nervous English was the birthright of the majority of preachers, men of affairs and letter writers in the seventeenth century, but Bunyan has the flair for selection and proper emphasis which marks the creative artist.

This is native eloquence, but when Bunyan came up to London to meet more learned Nonconformists like Benjamin Keach and John Owen he found that the colloquial manner, which was recommended in Bedford because it attracted hearers and made a stir in the country meeting-houses, was extolled for graver reasons. He found he was cast by natural circumstances to be an epitome of all the Puritan stylistic virtues. From the time of the first generation of Cambridge Puritans, they had declaimed against the vanity of humane rhetoric; the criterion of excellence was intelligibility and "speaking home in application" (as Samuel Clarke says of John Dod[28]). It may seem contradictory to speak of a Puritan literary tradition at all, when the men themselves consistently abused tradition, and praised in their favourite ministers the spontaneous, unselfconscious opening of the Word. But inevitably such terrorist attempts to abolish literature and reduce writing to all sense and no manner end by creating a new manner. The style of Puritan sermons is as easily recognizable as the baroque ornament of High Anglicans like Donne and Jeremy Taylor. It was signalized by the deliberate use of metaphors from common life and a concentration upon the "practical": the application of doctrine to personal experience. Bunyan and Arthur Dent, the other great provincial stylist of seventeenth-century Puritanism, fulfil the precepts of the Cambridge rhetoricians concerning the plain style, because they cannot write otherwise.

In great moments of drama Bunyan can heighten this style, and in these moments he can sometimes reproduce biblical rhythms. Yet in what is perhaps the finest of these scenes, the passage of the pilgrims over the river in the finale of Part Two, we are impressed chiefly by certain splendid phrases, not by a musical relation of all the parts. Valiant-for-Truth "passed over, and all the Trumpets sounded for him on the other side": this pulls out the diapason, and raises into poetry the sober dignity of his farewell speech. The daughter of Mr. Dispondencie "went through the River singing, but none could understand what she said": here the emphasis is brought about, as often, by understatement. It is dramatic writing, confident of its ability to convey these fine, nervous undertones, and not having to rely on a regularly rhythmical prose. On the other hand, Mr. Standfast's speech uses Hebrew parallelism which recalls the language of the Psalms and Canticles. There are, too, phrases like "die the death", and "caul of the heart", which recall Hebrew idiom as it is preserved in the Authorized Version, and still more in the Geneva Version. Such phrases satisfy Bunyan's preference for the particular and the concrete picture-phrase over any mere statement; the material picturesqueness of Old Testament style had a natural appeal for him. When Mr. Standfast says that the thought of the Celestial City beyond the water "doth lie as a glowing Coal at my Heart", though the tone of Hebrew poetry is recalled, the image is essentially Bunyan.

With its human richness, its mingling of moral dialogue and folk-tale adventure story, the First Part of *The Pilgrim's Progress* remains above all the allegory of the soul, the prisoner's tremendous attempt to find freedom for those inner experiences which the composition of *Grace Abounding* had revived in his mind. Like all first novels it is autobiographical. With the Second Part, and with *Badman* and *The Holy War* we enter a different world.

NOTES

CHAPTER IV

1. Brown, *John Bunyan*, pp. 239–48.
2. Joyce Godber, "The Imprisonments of John Bunyan", *Transactions of the Congregational Historical Society*, Vol. XVI, No. 1 (April 1949).
3. *Works*, ed. Offor, I, pp. 388–9.
4. Bunyan, *Works*, ed. Offor, III, pp. 382–92.
5. F. M. Harrison, *John Bunyan, a Record of Recent Research* (1940), MS. in Bunyan Library, Bedford, p. 63.
6. The view that *The Pilgrim's Progress* was written during the first imprisonment has already been suggested by Gwilym O. Griffith (in *John Bunyan*, 1927, pp. 224–5) and supported by F. M. Harrison. There is an acute discussion from a different point of view in Henri Talon, *John Bunyan, The Man and his Works* (1951), pp. 315–18.
7. *The Gentleman's Magazine* (1765), p. 168.
8. S. T. Coleridge, *Literary Remains* (1838), III, p. 398.
9. Calvin, *Institution chrestienne*, ed. Pannier (Paris, 1936), I, pp. 107–8; II, pp. 251–92; III, pp. 64–5.
10. C. H. Firth, *Essays Historical and Literary* (Oxford, 1938), p. 151. Talon, *Bunyan*, p. 153.
11. William Haller, *The Rise of Puritanism* (Columbia, 1938), pp. 152–4.
12. *Passadges of Mr. Dods* (1617. MS. in Dr. Williams's Library), pp. 213, 216–17.
13. Richard Sibbes, *The Bruised Reede and Smoaking Flax* (1632), p. 126.
14. Richard Sibbes, *Bowels Opened, or a discovery of the near and dear Love, Union, and Communion betwixt Christ and the Church*, The Third Edition (1648), p. 242.
15. Cf. Maurice Hussey, "Bunyan's Mr. Ignorance", *Modern Language Review*, Vol. XLIV (October 1949), pp. 483–9.
16. Cf. G. R. Owst, *Literature and the Pulpit in Medieval England* (Cambridge, 1933), pp. 104–5.
17. Thomas Adams, *Selected Sermons*, ed. W. H. Stowell (1847), p. 154.
18. Adams, *op. cit.*, p. 97.
19. Thomas Goodwin, *A Childe of Light Walking in Darknesse* (1636), p. 3.
20. Thomas Taylor, *The Highway to Happinesse* (in *Works*, 1659), p. 4.

21. William Perkins, *The Art of Prophecying* (in *Works*, Cambridge, 1609), II, p. 751; Richard Bernard, *The Faithfull Shepheard* (1609), pp. 65–6.

22. Richard Bernard, *The Isle of Man, or the Legall Proceedings in Manshire against Sin* (1627).

23. *Works*, ed. Offor, III, p. 711.

24. Cf. Rosemary Freeman, *English Emblem Books* (1948), pp. 206–28; Roger Sharrock, "Bunyan and the English Emblem Writers", *Review of English Studies*, Vol. XXI (April 1945), pp. 105–16.

25. Geffrey Whitney, *A Choice of Emblemes* (1586), p. 225.

26. *Works*, ed. Offor, III, p. 500.

27. *Life and Works of Mr. John Bunyan* (in *The Heavenly Footman*, ed. 1700), p. 72.

28. Samuel Clarke, *A General Martyrologie* (1677, "The Third Edition, corrected and enlarged"), p. 176.

MR. BADMAN

I

The Pilgrim's Progress contains incidental portraits of false professors and hypocrites, but worldly wickedness lies outside its range. Bunyan was now prompted by the success of the allegory to depict "The Life and Death of the Ungodly, and their travel from this world to *Hell*". He must have taken some trouble with *The Life and Death of Mr. Badman*, which appeared in 1680, since the only book published in the interval was the uninspired *Treatise of the Fear of God* (1679). *Mr. Badman* is even less like *The Pilgrim's Progress* than *Paradise Regain'd* is like *Paradise Lost*. As with Milton, the sequel, if sequel it can be called, deliberately eschews the imaginative daring of the earlier work, and falls back on a plainer and somewhat arid manner. There is a relaxation of dramatic tension in this story of the primrose path of the reprobate, prosed over at a comfortable remove by two old Puritans. The tale involved in their pious comment contains much hard, dry observation of manners, though it lacks the emotional heights and depths of its predecessor.

Like the elect souls of the pilgrimage, Badman is fixed in his course; men are given up to sin "because they are abhorred of God, and because abhorred, therefore they shall fall into the commission of it". Neither the narrative nor the moral interest of *The Pilgrim's Progress* is stultified by the doctrine of predestination, since the point of reference is the mind of Christian and for him the issue is always in doubt. But in *Badman* Bunyan makes no attempt to enter the mind of the central character: judgement is passed on him at the start, and his life is studied from the outside. The reason for what might otherwise seem to be a technical lapse lies in the fact that, for Bunyan, fiction has to be filtered through theology, and the characters he describes with intimate knowledge have to think as theologians; Christian and Hopeful hope for salvation, but Badman does not believe he is going to be damned: his own estimation of his life is in terms which fall quite outside the Puritan scheme. He is not a theologian, and it is this even more than his absolute wickedness which precludes him from enjoying the sympathy of Bunyan's art. On the other hand, the realistic effect which can be obtained from the external portrayal of particular sins, as in By-Ends and Worldly Wiseman, is blurred in Badman, who has to be a compendium of all the vices.

He begins young. His innate depravity is demonstrated by a childhood addiction to lying, stealing, swearing and sabbath-breaking. Bunyan may be recalling his shame at his own swearing and unlawful pastimes; in any case, he is following contemporary preaching convention. Since he has righteous parents to set him a good example, Badman is clearly feeling the pull of his own nature. He is apprenticed to a good master, an acquaintance of his father, and soon gets into bad company; whoring, drunkenness, and stealing from his master are now added to his other vices. He runs away to serve out his time with a master of like mind, who "when his passions and rage was over, would laugh at and make merry with the sins of his servant *Badman*". After completing his education in this household, he persuades his father to set him up in a shop of his own, where he can give free rein to his lusts, and allows his loose companions to make him the "jack-pay-for-all". But he is able to retrieve his losses by a rich marriage with an orphan of godly upbringing; his courtship is a consummate piece of play-acting by which he convinces her that his love for her good qualities has changed his manner of life.

Once married, he returns to his old ways, and when he is again burdened with debt he extricates himself by a false bankruptcy; he emerges from it with a handsome profit, having paid his creditors five shillings in the pound. He cheats his customers by various ingenious methods. He has weights to buy by and weights to sell by, measures to sell by and measures to buy by; with even more subtlety, he sometimes uses true weights and measures and a false balance, so that when customers complain he can swear his innocence and urge them to

take his weights to be proved. The only form of deceit in which
he does not excel is in making a show of religion, "for he was,
especially by those that dwelt near him, too well known to do
that, though he would bungle at it as well as he could". Sickness
rouses him to temporary remorse, but it springs from fear of
hell and not from genuine repentance; as soon as he is out of
danger he is ready to listen to the physician who tells him
that his fears and outcries were caused by lightheadedness.
His wife dies of a broken heart, and after a time he marries
another, who "to be plain . . . was a very whore, and had as
great resort came to her, where time and place was appointed,
as any of them all". After about fifteen years together, they
have sinned away all his substance, "and parted as poor as
Howlets". Badman dies of his excesses without repentance.
As a conclusion to a narrative filled with the violence and ugli-
ness of sin, the comparative ease of his death provides a fine
stroke of drama and indicates a soul completely lost to grace:

> Pray how was he in his death? was Death strong upon him? or
> did he dye with ease, quietly?
> As quietly as a Lamb.

Though Badman is meant to be a general type of the
reprobate, Bunyan has, by abandoning allegory, abandoned also
the effort to universalize his fable. The sins which receive the
most detailed treatment at the hands of the narrators are those
that are characteristic of Badman's calling. The novel is a
cautionary tale of middle-class commercial life in a provincial
town. The more intellectual vices find hardly any place: pride,
for instance, receives only a perfunctory treatment late in the
book. Bunyan was well aware of the traditional theological
classification according to which pride was the source of all
other moral corruption, "the master-pocke of the soul", as
his predecessor Arthur Dent had said,[1] but he allows an over-
riding concern with social morality to upset the proper theological structure of his sinner's progress. The Puritanism which had
sunk its roots in the retail trading class, and had moulded the
habits of its members, was already receiving a reciprocal
influence from the circumstances of life in a trading community.
Commercial dishonesty and offences against sexual respecta-

bility play the largest part in Badman's career. A change in Bunyan's interests had taken place in the early years of his pastorate; it is only faintly perceptible in the studies of heretics in the First Part of *The Pilgrim's Progress*; it leads him from the translation of the spiritual life into allegorical terms to the direct description of the life around him.

In spite of differences in property and status, the brethren of the Bedford church were predominantly shopkeepers and tradesmen. In 1670 they included, at the poorer end of the scale, a heel-maker, a shoemaker, a blacksmith and a pipemaker; more affluent members were a maltster, a grocer, a haberdasher, and a tanner who held the office of constable.[2] The congregation insisted on a high standard of social behaviour in its members. In 1674 days of prayer were appointed on account of the number of the brethren who had run into debt and were unable to meet their obligations, to the great scandal of the church. Similarly, in 1677, Edward Dent was ex-communicated for failing to satisfy his creditors.[3] The sins which received the sharpest condemnation were those likely to bring the holy community into public contempt in the larger society within which it was trying to find its niche. As well as dishonest dealing, personal immorality of the more sensational kind was punished; in addition to the case of John Rush the drunkard, there was some wife-beating, and one or two bad cases of sexual promiscuity, which had to be dealt with during Bunyan's period of office.

Not only were the brethren obliged to be in the vanguard of respectability; they also had to be protected against contamination from outside, and sustained in their resistance to official persecution. The church was still a society within a society, engaged in the process of leavening the whole lump. Under Bunyan's successor, Sister Gates was rebuked for marrying "a Carnall Man". Bunyan often had to warn members of his flock against becoming parties to such matches, and Badman's marriage with a "professor" is the occasion for a long digression on the subject:

It is a deadly thing, I see, to be unequally yoked with Unbelievers. If this woman had had a good Husband, how happily might they have lived together! Such an one would have prayed for her, taught her, and also would have encouraged her in the Faith, and Ways of God . . . she should have gone more warily to work . . . what if she had engaged a Godly Minister or two to have talked with *Mr. Badman*?

The voice of pastoral experience is again heard when Badman's reaction to pious and unwelcome sick-bed visitors is described in some detail: "he would often seem to fail in his spirits at the sight of them", would evade their questions about his spiritual condition, and finally would have them sent away with the excuse that he was sleeping. Badman's ill-treatment of his wife prevents her from attending the Sunday meeting, but he cannot bring himself to lay information against her Nonconformist friends, though he threatens to do so. The reason given is interesting: his business would suffer if he played the informer, which suggests that sympathy for the persecuted was general at this middle-class level; and this is borne out by the demonstrations in Bedford in 1670 against apparitors who tried to distrain Nonconformists' goods.[4]

Badman's composite wickedness is described, then, from the world Bunyan knew. It is still a transitional world, in which the religious devotee is to some extent separated from society. The class under observation has not yet reached the more settled bourgeois advancement it was to achieve in the age of Defoe. The informer watching the conventicle from a tree is still as much the villain as the shady or libidinous shopkeeper; the implication is that Badman is still partly conceived as the enemy of the saints, partly as a projection of the weaknesses to which the saints themselves are liable. Already the combination of fleshly lust and sharp practice gives us the first important literary example of the late Puritan principle that personal dissoluteness is bad for business: the old Puritan heroism is giving way in this parable to the new Nonconformist caution.

The social morality of the novel is also transitional. Bunyan's business ethic, like that of Richard Baxter, retains many medieval features, as might be expected from the precepts enunciated in *Christian Behaviour*. He denounces extortion by middlemen who buy corn to force up prices at a time of scarcity;

this is the sin of making the shekel great mentioned in the prophet Amos; and he considers in medieval fashion that the dealer in provisions has a duty to the poor:

> Be also moderate in all thy sellings, and be sure let the poor have a pennyworth, and sell thy Corn to those in necessity: Which then thou wilt do, when thou shewest mercy to the poor in thy selling to him, and when thou for his sake, because he is poor, undersellest the market.

Usury is condemned, as it was by other Puritan authorities. The poor are still the especial children of God:

> A poor condition has preventing mercy attending of it. The poor, because they are poor, are not capable of sinning against God as the rich man does. . . .
> All that a man has over and above what serves for his present necessity and supply, serves only to feed the lusts of the eye. . . .

At the same time, the doctrine of the just price has given way to the idea of the competitive market ("all things that we buy and sell, do ebbe and flow, as to price, like the Tide"); and Bunyan is vague about how the market should be controlled in the interests of economic justice. The literary consequence is a certain ambiguity in the economic aspect of Badman's wickedness. When he prospers, his wealth is a token of his inability to go through the eye of the needle: Bunyan's conservatism is in the ascendent. But sometimes the stress is laid on Badman's misapplication of riches and the disorderly conduct of his affairs, and then the point of view of his creator is that of the shopkeeper or producer with his religious criterion imperceptibly shading off into a standard of efficiency. It is significant that Badman's second wife enables him to run through most of his money, and at his death he is apparently reduced in circumstances, though there is no clear-cut attempt to point a moral by suggesting that this is a punishment for his sins.

However, Bunyan's strongest sympathy is reserved for the poor villager who lives far from the market, and depends, since he cannot afford to lose a day's work, on an extortionate

retailer for his butter and cheese. Though his parable explores
some of the new problems of the market, his heart remains in
the simple village economy where the consumer's needs came
first. The complete acceptance of a money economy, found a
generation later in the novels of Defoe, is truer to the actual
development of Dissent, and utterly alien to Bunyan's way of
thought.

II

The story is told in the form of a dialogue between Mr.
Wiseman and Mr. Attentive. By this method of narration the
real action is set at a distance from the reader and interrupted
by lengthy digressions. Bunyan took the idea of a dialogue from
Arthur Dent's *Plaine Mans Path-way*; he had already explored
some of its possibilities in the conversational passages of *The
Pilgrim's Progress*. Dent gives "eight signs of salvation" and
"nine manifest signs of condemnation", which are the source
of similar catalogues in *Badman*; and both Dent and Bunyan
deal at length with some of the well-worn themes of popular
homily, such as drunkenness, swearing, and excessive finery in
dress;[5] they declaim against women "with their Bulls-foretops
(head-dresses), with their naked shoulders, and Paps hanging
out like a Cows bag". More than any early Puritan homiletic
writer, Dent shares Bunyan's raciness of style and his command
of popular proverbs. "And so they brought their Noble to
Ninepence," says Wiseman, describing the extravagance of
Badman and his second wife. The standard of reasonable
conduct laid down in the book is supported as much by these
dogmatic propositions of popular culture as by Biblical
references, and as a result one has the impression that Wiseman
is pronouncing the common judgement of the folk rather than
the voice of theological authority. The principle that masters
and parents should tread carefully in front of their children and
servants is enforced by the merely prudential maxim: "Hedges
have eyes and little Pitchers have ears."

Dent's book is a homily with a very thin story, and Bunyan
has gone some way towards turning his novel into a sermon.
When Wiseman is allowed to develop any topic at length, the

style loses the colloquial quality of the shorter interchanges with Attentive, and assumes the rhetorical manner of the prose treatises. The pauses and repetitions of the orator begin to appear:

> Soon after such marriages, Conviction (the first step toward heaven) hath ceased; Prayer (the next step toward heaven) hath ceased; Hungrings and thirstings after salvation (another step towards the Kingdom of Heaven) have ceased.

Wiseman is certainly Bunyan himself, and a personal habit of discourse may provide some justification for the blending of talk and preaching. He tells a story about the time when he was in prison which must be a personal recollection, and there is a blood-curdling anecdote of demonic possession, as seen through the eyes of a terrified small boy, which must go back to Bunyan's childhood. But the dialogue framework is clumsily managed: each phase of Badman's life produces a digression, and many of the episodes are inartistically and even inconsistently linked to the main narrative. Attentive asks for a discourse on how a bad master may corrupt his apprentices, when Badman is still with his first master, who was blameless, and he gets it. The two long stories about informers are not stricly relevant, since Badman never becomes an informer, but only threatens to do so. Attentive, who is tediously ready with the appropriate comment, sometimes shows as much knowledge of the story as Wiseman, who is supposed to be telling it to him, and at one point naïvely excuses what can only be Bunyan's own slackness of grip on the dialogue by saying: "I take the liberty to speak thus of Mr. Badman, upon a confidence of what you, Sir, have said of him is true."

This is unconscious humour, but there are some deliberate and not unsuccessful attempts to sugar the pill. Though the differentiation of the two speakers is not pursued very far, Attentive is the foil to Wiseman, and seems to be a younger and less distinguished professor, whose eagerness to say the right thing often incurs a snub:

> Attentive: If you please, let us return again to Mr. Badman himself, if you have any more to say of him.

H

Wiseman: More! We have scarce throughly begun with *Any thing* that we have said.

And there is the occasion when Attentive, not always able to supply a fresh response as the tale of depravity lengthens, can only manage "This Badman was a sad wretch", and is put in his place by Wiseman with the tart remark, "Thus you have often said before". Equally diverting is Attentive's persistent and continually frustrated desire to learn the manner of Badman's death; ever after learning that his death was the reason for the great sigh Wiseman heaved at the beginning of their conversation, he is determined to get to the bottom of it, but before his wish is granted, he has to endure the dead man's biography from childhood onwards. Often he recurs politely to his main concern, but is firmly put off by his mentor:

Attentive: Well, Sir, now I have heard enough of Mr. Badman's naughtiness, pray now proceed to his Death.
Wiseman: Why Sir, the Sun is not so low, we have yet three hours to night.
Attentive: . . . but I thought you had even now done with his life.
Wiseman: Done! no, I have yet much more to say.

In a sense the whole gradual unfolding of the story, with its interpolated moral essays and additional anecdotes, is a preparation for the starkly simple account of this death—"as quietly as a Lamb". [6] But the additional stories have an effect of their own; they are, as it were, in the forefront of the narrative, because Wiseman and Attentive often vouch for them with their own eyes, whereas much of Badman's career, indeed the most important episodes in it, like his marriage, and his bankruptcy, are reported on from hearsay. There are about twenty-five of these anecdotes, many of them not more than a few sentences in length, and told with extreme conciseness. The purpose of all of them is to strike terror; the warning of Badman's career is mitigated by more detailed moral instruction on the obligations of commerce and family life, but these choric illustrations aim at nothing but immediate and lurid terror. They take up the theme of Bunyan's scarifying sermons, and they belong to a definite genus of Puritan religious instruction: the literature of judgements. This class of writings, dealing with divine vengeances upon the wicked, probably originated in the *exempla* of the medieval sermon. Fearful judgements of this kind against the reprobate, like the providential escapes or revelations mentioned in the biographies of the saints, appealed to the active spirit of Calvinists, who sought to detect the pattern of the divine purpose at work in a fallen world to bless, to punish, and to create the community of the church. In the earlier seventeenth century, that age of popularization, encyclopaedic collections of such anecdotes began to be compiled for the general reader. Thomas Beard's *Theatre of God's Judgments* was a well-known work; John Reynolds's *The Triumphs of Gods Revenge against the crying and execrable Sinne of Murther* (1621), embellished with fearsome woodcuts, satisfied the popular demand for stories of murder and passion as well as of judgements. Bunyan's main source is a later compilation, Samuel Clark's *A Mirrour and Looking-glass for both Saints and Sinners.*[7] He acknowledges his debt to Clark for several of the stories in *Badman.* The account of Dorothy Matley, for instance, a Derbyshire woman who forswore herself and was swallowed up in the earth, is expanded from a rather meagre version in Clark. Bunyan adds many circumstantial details about her work in the lead mines, her theft from the boy with whom she was working, who "had laid his breeches by" with the money in them, and tells how her tub and sieve twirled round and round in the earth and mysteriously disappeared. Thus the naturalistic background of concrete objects and measurements is developed in a manner which anticipates Defoe: it is the confidence trickster's method of purveying the marvellous.

Some of the other judgement stories are drawn from personal experience, like that of the desperate H. S. who said, "What would the devil do for company, if it were not for such as I?" He is Harry, one of the wild companions of the young Bunyan at Elstow, who is also encountered in *Grace Abounding.* But many told at second hand or derived from oral tradition are redeemed from the crudity of the moral purpose by the art with which they are related. The tale of old Tod, the thief who repented and gave himself up to justice, is one of these:

At a Summer Assizes holden at Hartfort, while the Judge was sitting upon the Bench, comes this old *Tod* into the Court, cloathed in a green Suit, with his Leathern Girdle in his hand, his Bosom open, and all on a dung sweat, as if he had run for his Life; and being come in he spake aloud as follows: *My Lord, Here is the veryest Rogue that breaths upon the face of the earth.*

The interest is all in the dramatic entrance and the physical detail; Tod remains an external figure, as he was seen by the crowd in the court, but he comes a little closer than Badman. The virtue of the detail is not symbolic, as in *The Pilgrim's Progress*, but solidly materialistic; Tod's green suit and his sweat convey only the immediacy of an eye-witness account. Even the moral of these stories has something materialistic and pagan about it. Though the judgements are supposed to show the wrath of God, it is usually the devil, and a violent, cloven-footed devil of folk tradition, who carries off the victims. At the climax the spiritual is at a discount: the stress is upon violent and disgusting physical dissolution. The tavern-keeper enters the room to find his guest gone and the iron bars in the window bent and bloody. A blasphemer is torn into four pieces in the air and the pieces scattered on four high-ways. The atmosphere here is not that of Christian morality, but recalls the primitive folk tale terror of M. R. James's ghost stories. In so far as an implied rule of conduct does emerge, it is a naturalistic one, the voice of popular experience: offences against nature or inordinate indulgence bring their own retribution. Through the chinks in the Calvinist scheme we catch glimpses of the unedifying prudential world of common life, which has for its precepts the proverb rather than the Bible. When Wiseman relates how Badman, after trying for a long time to avoid a second marriage, at last met "one was too hard for him", he speaks with the voice not of sacred, but of worldly wisdom.

Mr. Badman is Bunyan's nearest approach to the novel: it has in flashes both the realism—the cult of verisimilitude for its own sake—and the secular view of life which were to be the great instruments of the eighteenth-century novel. But Bunyan was not working at high pressure in it; he had found an edifying form for the satisfaction of impulses towards the sensational and the marvellous which in his unregenerate days had been appeased by the chap-books of Stourbridge Fair. Unlike its predecessor, *Badman* can be read as mere entertainment under a mask of piety. To note its obvious anticipation of Defoe is beside the point unless the radical difference is also perceived. Defoe has a consistent and completely secularized view of life; Bunyan's blend of Puritan exhortation, middle-class ethic, and folk attitudes is part compromise, part confusion. His own stand remains clear and he did not choose to follow any further in the direction he found necessary for this entertainment. But, though it lacks the seriousness and universality of *The Pilgrim's Progress*, it is too well written to be handed over to the social historian, however much its merits may have been exaggerated by the enthusiasts of realism.

NOTES

CHAPTER V

1. *The Plaine Mans Path-way to Heaven*, p. 33.
2. These particulars are found in *A True and Impartiall Narrative of Some Illegal and Arbitrary proceedings . . . in and near the Town of Bedford* (1670), pp. 3–12.
3. *Church Book*, pp. 54, 66.
4. *A true and Impartiall Narrative*, passim.
5. *The Plaine Mans Path-way to Heaven*, pp. 40–4, 138–49.
6. The idea of the quiet end of the wicked is also met in Thomas Fuller's account of the Duke of Alva: "But Gods justice on offenders goes not alwayes in the same path, nor the same pace: And he is not pardoned for the fault, who is for a while reprived from the punishment; yea sometimes the guest in the inne goes quietly to bed, before the reckoning for his supper is brought to him to discharge" (*The Profane State*, 1642, p. 441).
7. Clark's book was first published in 1646, and went through a number of editions in each of which fresh examples were added.

THE CHRISTIAN WARFARE

I

BUNYAN published nothing between *Badman* in 1680 and *The Holy War* in 1682. The interval is unusual for him and suggests that he was giving his whole attention to the new allegory; there is internal evidence, too, that it was more deeply meditated than any previous work. The book bore the imprint of two publishers who had not handled his work before.

Bunyan now turned to the second great metaphor of Christian experience. Less universal than the image of the human pilgrimage through life, the theme of spiritual conflict is yet traceable from the very beginnings of Christian preaching and poetry. St. Paul's description of the whole armour of God in the sixth chapter of the *Epistle to the Ephesians* is probably the source for much later allegory. The idea of a warfare in the soul between personified virtues and vices appears in the *Psychomachia* of Prudentius in the fourth century. In the middle ages it became part of the stock-in-trade of the popular sermon and was developed in further detail by Langland and by the authors of some of the morality plays. In the fifteenth-century *Castle of Perseverance* the human soul is besieged in a castle by the seven deadly sins and defended by the virtues, with symbolic roses as ammunition. Spenser relates the siege of the House of Alma, and Richard Bernard, Bunyan's predecessor in Puritan fiction, had employed the metaphor of a state or community for the individual soul.[1] All these elements are gathered together in *The Holy War*: the opposition of characters like Goodhope and Charity to Incredulity and Carnal Security; the very ancient conception of human nature as a little kingdom; the change of allegiance from God to Satan on the part of characters like Understanding and Conscience; and the siege to represent the assaults of temptation. Bunyan was ignorant of the long history behind the military image, though he had probably read Bernard's book; but the idea was everywhere in Puritan litera- ture, and in the everyday habits of exhortation with which he was familiar; it lay at the heart of Puritan mythology. Already, in *A Treatise of the Fear of God*, he had developed in an extended simile the conception of the heart as the chief fortress of the soul, which, if well manned, could keep the rest of the town in subjection to its rightful prince.[2]

To see life figuratively as a continual conflict with the powers of darkness, and the soul as a battleground of rival loyalties, a city which may at any moment be divided against itself, is to emphasize the more melodramatic implications of Christian belief. The military allegory can render admirably the great crises of the spiritual life, but as a vehicle for the general course of human existence it suffers from self-con- sciousness and over-intensity. To say this is to stumble over the uncertain verge of literary criticism and pass a judgement on the Puritan spirit. The journey metaphor is faithful to the variety and unexpectedness of human life and the metaphor of a military campaign is not; in *The Pilgrim's Progress* the fights with the monsters fall into proper proportion alongside episodes in which Christian and his companions gossip together or stroll across the pleasant plain called Ease. Also, the pilgrims have to contend with the neutral stubbornness of the natural world, as represented by the Hill Difficulty; the war allegory, by reducing everything to black and white, reflects the Calvinist tendency to abolish nature.

On the other hand, if in turning from one metaphor to the other Bunyan had to some extent to restrict his own sense of human reality, he did so in complete accordance with the earlier phases of his religious vision. He abandoned Bedfordshire, but returned to the terrible private universe of his Elstow days, when voices contended against voices, and his own mind, even at times his physical frame, was a country torn apart by civil strife. The frontispiece to the first edition shows a full-length portrait of Bunyan imposed on a miniature of the town of Mansoul, so that the buildings of the town can be seen through his body, and a fortress labelled "Heart Castle" is visible at his left breast.[3]

The personal element is also stressed in the prefatory verses; Bunyan presents his credentials to the reader as an eye-witness who was present in the thick of the fight:

> Let no men then count me a Fable-maker,
> Nor make my name or credit a partaker
> Of their derision: what is here in view
> Of mine own knowledg, I dare say is true.
>   I saw the Princes armed men come down
> By troops, by thousands, to besiege the Town.
> I saw the Captains, heard the Trumpets sound,
> And how his forces cover'd all the ground.
> Yea, how they set themselves in battel-ray,
> I shall remember to my dying day.
>   I saw the Colours waving in the wind. . . .

Clearly, *The Holy War* was intended primarily as yet another exploration of his own personal experience. But its keynote is the detached, almost scholastic re-interpretation of the experience in terms of military and political allegory. It is an ambitious book which tries to do much more than to allegorize his conversion and subsequent temptations. The First Part of *The Pilgrim's Progress* had aimed at a more modest goal and achieved an unexpected universality. Now Bunyan was attempting to make his symbols apply to the religious life of all mankind. Though he shows no signs of being spoilt by fame, he has become the self-conscious writer; no longer can he say "as I pulled, it came"; he has the obligation to make a book which shall not fall below the previous "best-seller", and a feeling of responsibility towards his fellow-sectaries. For the untutored genius of Bunyan there were obviously dangers here, but it is too easy to assume that under these conditions he was bound to produce an inferior book. A certain kind of book, what one is tempted to describe as the typical second novel, was likely to be written, one aiming higher than the first, and more literary than autobiographical in treatment. Bunyan seeks to provide at the popular level the equivalent of an heroic subject treated in the grand manner. As for the poet of literary epic, a certain degree of detachment is necessary; he is no longer the dreamer, but an observer, and the new attitude of grandeur and universality is struck in the first paragraph, just as the first words of *The Pilgrim's Progress* create the atmosphere of visionary immediacy:

> In my Travels, as I walked through many Regions and Countries, it was my chance to happen into that famous *Continent* of *Universe*; a very large and spacious Countrey it is. It lieth between the two Poles, and just amidst the four points of the Heavens. It is a place well watered, and richly adorned with Hills and Valleys, bravely situate; and for the most part (at least where I was) very fruitful, also well peopled, and a very sweet Air. . . .
>
> I learned much of their mother-tongue, together with the Customs, and manners of them among whom I was. . . . Yea I had (to be sure) even lived and died a Native among them (so was I taken with them and their doings) had not my Master sent for me home to his House, there to do business for him and to over-see business done.

By receiving an assurance that he is one of the elect, Bunyan is carried above the spacious country of universe and the corporation of Mansoul, so that he can regard them with a sublime detachment. After the first paragraph, the "I saw", "I beheld", of the visionary, so constant in the earlier allegory, are absent. No dreamer awakes at the end of the book; with the first person narrator forgotten, Christ addresses Mansoul in a conclusion of epic splendour.

II

Bunyan begins with an account of the fall of Satan and the rebel angels, and their resolve to revenge themselves by seizing the newly created town of Mansoul, "one of the chief works and delights of King Shaddai" (he uses this Hebrew name for God the Father). An infernal council is held to decide how best to accomplish this. The resemblance to *Paradise Lost* is rather startling; possibly one of Bunyan's more learned London friends may have introduced him to Milton's poem, and the debate in Pandemonium caught his fancy.[4] Further evidence of epic pretensions is provided

by the inclusion among the devils of the classical furies Alecto
and Tisiphone, as well as Lucifer, Beelzebub and Apollyon;
their chief is also given a recondite name—Diabolus.

Diabolus asserts his claim to approach the town alone and
try to win it by guile. On the advice of Lucifer he assumes the
shape of a dragon, "for that he was in those days as familiar
with the Town of *Mansoul* as now is the bird with the Boy".
Thus Bunyan's enthusiasm for the high argument of the Fall
involves him in a difficulty at the start. The creation and the
fall of the angels have been described directly without allegory;
then when Diabolus presents himself before Mansoul there is
a clumsy attempt to combine the Biblical story of the tree of
knowledge with the siege metaphor: Ill-Pause, Diabolus's
orator, harangues the citizens who are on the walls and
persuades them to eat the fruit; Captain Resistance is slain,
and my Lord Innocency dies "by the stinking breath of that
Treacherous Villain".

When however Diabolus has gained admission into the town
and reorganized the corporation, the allegory begins to operate
on two levels at once. Mansoul is still mankind, now fallen, but
it is also an individual soul hardened by original sin and waiting
for grace. The fusion of psychological and historical allegory
was no doubt made easier by the tendency, which Bunyan
shared with other left-wing sectaries, especially the Quakers,
and which is exemplified in *Grace Abounding*, to treat God's
dealings with Israel, and indeed the whole Old Testament
narrative, as an analogue of the soul's history.[5] Most of the
civic officials fit more suitably into the personal allegory: the
Conscience is Mr. Recorder, whose place is now taken by Mr.
Forget-good, though his thundering voice can still make
Mansoul tremble; Diabolus builds a tower to shut out the sun
from the Lord Mayor's house (the understanding is darkened)
and puts a new Lord Mayor, the Lord Lustings, in his place;
and the Lord Wilbewill, who represents human freewill, takes
service under the new governor. But because of what has
gone before, Bunyan is irretrievably committed, too, to an
epic of the religious history of mankind. As the vast canvas un-
rolls, we see the same allegory sustaining the narrative of the
Redemption as well as the saga of an individual conversion.

Shaddai hears the news of the surrender of his beloved Mansoul, and he accepts the offer of his son Emanuel to recover the town. First he sends an army of forty thousand men representing the terrors of the Mosaic law; their captains are Boanerges, who signifies powerful preaching (for the classic spiritual history begins with an awakening sermon), Conviction, Judgement and Execution. Their attacks cause the townspeople to begin to repent of their rebellion, and a loyalist party under Understanding and Conscience is able to make some headway; but after Diabolus's proposals for a truce have been rejected, it is only Emanuel himself with a fresh army who is able to take the town. After many petitions the inhabitants receive a free pardon from their prince; the corporation is new modelled, the Diabolonians who corrupted the town are tried and condemned, and Emanuel appoints his Chief Secretary (the Holy Spirit) to be the principal preacher.

So far Bunyan has described, at the level of world history, the Old Testament period, the Redemption, and the founding of the primitive church. At the psychological level, these correspond to the awakening of the soul by sermons, conviction of sin, the attempt to live a merely moral life, fresh despair, and finally the knowledge of justification by Christ's intercession, obtained only after a long period of prayer, and followed by the commencement of the work of sanctification in the soul. But his ambition still soared. It is as if Milton had trebled the size of his epic of the Fall, so as to take in the Redemption and the whole sweep of Christian history culminating in the last days described in the Book of Revelation; and this would be to leave out of account the holy war within the soul which is kept in the forefront of the story. After the liberation of Mansoul just under half yet remains to be told. Diabolonians still lurk in the town, and Mr. Carnal Security is a particularly dangerous fifth columnist. Emanuel leaves (which signifies both the backsliding of the individual and the decline of the church), and the Diabolonians begin to plan another campaign. Two hosts are sent against the town, one of Doubters under Incredulity, and one of Bloodmen or persecutors. After further struggles, Emanuel relieves Mansoul a second time, and exhorts the inhabitants to hold fast until his final coming.

The interpretation of the later events is less simple, except at the psychological level, where, as in *The Pilgrim's Progress*, the order of experiences in *Grace Abounding* is the best guide. Once more the long period of spiritual doubt is recapitulated, with its "very great storm" of temptations. It is noteworthy that the Doubters do not represent intellectual questionings of belief, but different forms of despair concerning salvation; their nine companies are enumerated, and they include the Election-doubters, the Vocation-doubters, the Grace-doubters, and so on. Their long and dangerous attack is delivered when the citizens have become carnally secure, "all taken with the words of this tattling Diabolonian gentleman". An important marginal note at this point says, "'Tis not Grace received, but Grace improved, that preserves the soul from temporal dangers": the Mansoulians have neglected to improve their talent, and when they awake to the danger Christ has departed, they have forgotten the promises previously declared to them, and have in their remorse become an easy prey to the Doubters. It is the story of Doubting Castle over again. As in Bunyan's conversion, when the Doubters force their way into the town, they strike terror by their blasphemies:

Oh the fearful state of *Mansoul now*! now every corner swarmed with outlandish *Doubters*; Red-coats and Black-coats, walked the Town by clusters, and filled up all the houses with hideous noises, vain Songs, lying stories and blasphemous language against *Shaddai* and his Son.

The statement that the occupation of the town and the siege of Heart Castle, which holds out until Emanuel's arrival, lasted "about two years and a half", may be a piece of auto-biography. After a short interval, the Bloodmen succeed the Doubters, just as Bunyan passed in *Grace Abounding* from his spiritual doubts to the legal persecution of his imprisonment, with a very brief account of his ministry. Emanuel's second liberation of the town is, in terms of the allegory of the soul, a final assurance of grace; prayer has at last been answered; however, the life of the believer is not yet over; Carnal Sense and Unbelief still remain within the walls (a typically Calvinist comment on the last stages of sanctification); the citizens are adjured by Emanuel to keep their white garments spotless, and bidden "Hold fast till I come."

The complication of the later episodes is caused by the introduction of a fifth monarchy theme, which almost amounts to a third level of the allegory. As Bunyan becomes more and more immersed in recounting battles and sieges, he is stirred by a deep nostalgia for his own military past. This leads him to recollect also the millenarian hopes of the early years of the Bedford church, so strong among Baptists like Gifford and himself who had served in the army. He concludes his history of the Christian church with a partial exposition of the events of the last days, as symbolized in Revelation and extensively commented on by some of his fellow-sectaries. To add to the confusion, a strand of political allegory dealing with contemporary events appears in this part of the book; the Bloodmen are intended to represent the persecutors of Nonconformists under Charles II. A ramification of this fourth allegorical theme satirizes the plan for remodelling Bedford corporation in 1681.

It is not necessary to suppose that these complex layers of significance are simply due to confusion of purpose; Bunyan, like Spenser, understood the technique of multiple allegory; he is a late representative of the tradition, but he had acquired it from the source which inspired the middle ages: Biblical exegesis. Though Puritans held the general Protestant belief in the supremacy of the literal sense, they employed the relics of the old fourfold interpretation on books like Canticles and Revelation, where only an allegorical method would be satisfactory. In the posthumously published *Exposition on the First Ten Chapters of Genesis*, Bunyan detects one literal and three allegorical meanings as being present in the text at the same time; the flood is of course a real event, but it is also a type of the enemies of the church, of water baptism under the New Testament, and finally "of the last and general overthrow of the world by fire and brimstone".[6]

The Fifth Monarchy agitators of the Commonwealth period thought that the Stuart rule, and after that the Protectorate, was the continuation of the fourth or Roman monarchy, which was only to be ended by the advent of King Jesus. In

Revelation the fourth monarchy is the reign of the Beast,
and the corresponding era in *The Holy War* is the period of
Mansoul's corruption under Carnal Security and the assaults
of the Doubters and Bloodmen. The high-water mark of
persecution, when the Doubters break into the town, may be the
slaying of the witnesses (Rev. xi). Emanuel's second liberation
would be the millenium (the renewal of the citizens' white
garments is one among many hints from Revelation), and the
last attack of the Bloodmen would be the warfare associated
with Gog and Magog:

> And when the thousand years are expired, Satan shall be
> loosed out of his prison.
> And shall go out to deceive the nations which are in the four
> quarters of the earth, Gog and Magog, to gather them together
> to battle: the number of whom is as the sand of the sea.
> And they went up on the breadth of the earth, and compassed
> the camp of the saints about, and the beloved city; and fire came
> down from God out of heaven, and devoured them.
>
> (Rev. xx, 7–9).

However, the extraordinary poetry of Revelation, with its
swift movement from one vision to another, makes it just as
difficult for the reader to discern how another allegorist
interpreted its revolutions as it was for the political Fifth
Monarchy men to apply its chronology to contemporary events.

There are many glances at current history, but they hardly
amount to a distinct level of the allegory; only in the section
dealing with the Bloodmen does there seem to be any continuity
of reference to historical events. The appointment by Diabolus
of Mr. Filth, who encourages the publication of wanton songs
and ballads, is a hit at Roger L'Estrange, who, as licenser of the
press, was particularly severe on Nonconformist writers and
publishers, and was also noted for the scurrility of his own
pamphlets. In the period of the Doubters the city is stricken by
plague; and some time afterwards a Diabolonian plot is detected
by Mr. Prywell in circumstances which recall informers'
reports of the Popish Plot: he hears a murmuring "at a place
called Vile-hill", and draws near to eavesdrop on the con-
spirators. Then there is a most interesting contemporary

allusion to the dangers of bourgeois prosperity for Nonconformists, when, at a second council of devils, Lucifer advocates
that, as a prelude to a second campaign, the town shall be
allowed to grow rich. Mr. Penniwise-Pound-foolish and Mr.
Get-ith'-hundred-and-lose-ith'-shire are to be sent among the
burgesses, who will become taken up with much business and
surfeited with the good things of the world. As in *Badman*,
there is here a criticism of a Puritanism which was becoming
less theologically earnest and more commercially complacent.

The complexity of allusion in *The Holy War* is impressive,
but it deprives the work of intimacy. There is a huge gallery of
characters whom we admire in turn for the skill which has
woven them into the pattern, but none who has more than one
dimension; even the engagingly swashbuckling Lord Wilbewill
remains a theological abstraction varnished over to look like a
Restoration milord. Alongside flesh and blood characters like
Greatheart and Old Honest, whom Bunyan was to create only a
year or so after he had written *The Holy War*, they are pale
shadows. He had not lost the gift for combining living people
and scenes with his "similitudes", but the cosmic structure of
The Holy War, which had so thrilled his imagination, afforded
him no opportunity. In the phrase Walter Bagehot applied to
Paradise Lost, the Christian warfare had to be reduced to a
political transaction, and Bunyan was without the experience of
affairs which enabled Milton to enrich the debates in his
second book. He lacked the literary professional's techniques
for describing courts and camps. He did however know something about municipal politics: in 1681 Charles II began to put
into action his policy for obtaining control of the corporate
towns, where Whigs and Nonconformists were firmly en-
trenched, by imposing new charters. At Bedford two civic
officials unfavourable to the royal interest were removed on an
allegation that they had condoned seditious conventicles.[7]
The conventicles were probably Bunyan's, and no doubt he
watched the movement of events with vigilance; for in *The
Holy War* he gives a remarkably accurate forecast of the gradual
downfall of the corporation. Bedford, like London, had its
new charter in 1684, after it had been packed with new burgesses
whose votes could be trusted, and Diabolus's first reign in

Mansoul begins with a similar new modelling of the town.
New aldermen are created, as well as a new Lord Mayor and
Recorder, and an oath of exclusive loyalty to Diabolus is
imposed, resembling the oath of allegiance or a religious test.
After Emanuel's restoration there is another new modelling;
a new charter is granted, and the text of it is given in full: it
represents in theological terms the new covenant of forgiveness
through Christ's blood, and takes the place of the former
charter which was the old law of the ten commandments.
This climax in the story is given the warmth and colour of a
nine days' wonder in Bedford town, and, as is customary in the
exalted moments of Bunyan's history, there is the accompani-
ment of music and bell ringing:

> But what joy! what comfort! what consolation think you, did now
> possess the hearts of the men of *Mansoul*; the Bells ringed, the
> Minstrils played, the people danced, the Captains shouted, the
> Colours waved in the wind, and the silver Trumpets sounded.

This is both the supreme moment of grace, when, in his own
experience, Bunyan had seen "evidence, as I thought, of my
Salvation from Heaven, with mary golden Seals thereon", and
the historical moment of the Redemption. The most genuine
notes in *The Holy War* are struck when he is able to turn the
political transaction into a parochial transaction, and the
municipal changes of Mansoul are better material for this
than the epic battles and debates.

III

The attempt at a complex and allusive grandeur tends to
defeat itself. None of the military devils can create an atmosphere
of terror like that of the Valley of the Shadow of Death, nor does
Emanuel's triumphal pageantry breathe that sense of the
numinous suggested by the Delectable Mountains or by the
unseen world across the river, while Bunyan's humanity,
parcelled out among scores of characters, has only a tiny drop
for each. The dramatic interest is broken up by Emanuel's

two relief expeditions, neither of which is a true climax, since final salvation lies outside the fable. Theology has certainly allowed no nonsense from art. It is impossible to endorse Macaulay's judgement that *The Holy War* would have been our greatest allegory if *The Pilgrim's Progress* had never been written. That place would surely be occupied by *Piers Plowman*. Yet to think of Langland is suddenly to have brought home to one how near Bunyan comes to his achievement. Their problems and methods are the same. Langland too presents a multiple allegory; he too abounds in minor allegorical personages, who illustrate no important theme, but exist only to colour straight-forward actions (like Bunyan's Mr. Wouldlive who draws up the petition for mercy sent to Emanuel); both writers, in half their metaphors, seem never to stray far from the margin of the Bible; both leave the story unfinished, but Langland has that extra grace of the imagination which makes a virtue of his abrupt conclusion by suggesting a symbolism of the Christian life which has no ending on this side of the grave.

If one misses the higher imaginative flights in *The Holy War;* there is ample recompense in the realism and humour of certain episodes. But before turning to them, tribute should be paid to the skill with which every detail of the huge theological structure is translated into some allegorical incident or character. One must remember that Bunyan was looking for safe and exact equivalents which would not pervert his doctrine, as well as lively representations of the doctrine. The most interesting phases of the allegory are those involving some degree of tension between symbol and idea. The citizens of Mansoul are free agents, and their great man, Wilbewill, has a romantic independence about him which tinges the purity of Calvinist doctrine with a Pelagian streak; when he takes service under Diabolus he demonstrates the *corruptio optimi*, only to redeem himself by exemplary courage during the second siege. But, after all, there is nothing strictly incompatible with Bunyan's doctrine; it is simply that the stresses of theology are bound to be different when dogma is transferred to fiction: Satan steals the limelight, and the unregenerate Wilbewill has a similar tarnished splendour, because they are characters who act and make decisions. The sanctified will is able to curb the affections only through

I

the assistance of grace; but when this principle is coaxed into the fable it has a different effect and makes Wilbewill seem rather a fine fellow:

> The Lord *Wilbewill* also, he took the charge of watching **against** the Rebels within . . . ever since he took penance for his fault, he has showed as much honesty and bravery of spirit as any he in *Mansoul*.

Elsewhere the predominant impression is of the ingenuity with which the doctrinal points are made. Ear-gate is the vital gate of the town. Tradition, Human-wisdom and Man's Invention enlist in Shaddai's army, but when taken prisoners readily change sides: here is the mechanic preacher's jaundiced comment on beneficed turncoats like Edward Fowler, delivered in a little excursus in the manner of Langland, a gargoyle having nothing to do with the main structure of the work. The strict doctrine of grace is amply recompensed for any intruding liberalism when Emanuel, after an inscrutable rejection of numerous petitions, grants by his full pardon an entirely undeserved mercy to the rebel town. Emanuel's army has "forty-four battering rams and twelve slings, to whirl stones withal" (the books of the Old and New Testament); and the word of attack is "Ye must be born again". Then, when Diabolus attempts to negotiate, Emanuel argues that Mansoul is his by purchase, and refuses to consider any proposals for a truce; the Devil, now transformed, in Paul's words which Bunyan remembered, into an angel of light, is prepared even to establish and maintain "a sufficient ministry, besides lectures, in Mansoul", but it will not do; the reflection on the established church is clear enough. Throughout there is the play of an ever alert intellectual skill in building analogies, as well as the accustomed shrewdness of observation. Only rarely does there appear to be an unbridgeable emotional gap between the idea and the similitude, and then Bunyan has usually been betrayed by his absolute trust in the language of the Bible. Thus, because Paul in the *Epistle to the Galatians*, speaks of crucifying the affections and lusts, the condemned Diabolonians are put to death by a literal crucifixion; it is a token of his naïveté, not of his ferocity, that Bunyan was led astray in this manner.

Allegorical competence is combined with realism and humour in the trial of the Diabolonians to raise that episode well above the general level of narrative interest. Necessity had given Bunyan a good working knowledge of court procedure, and he also had before him as a model a previous allegorical trial of vices in Bernard's *Isle of Man*. The prisoners are brought in "pinioned and chained together as the custom of the Town of *Mansoul* was". It was also the English practice in treason cases. The pleas are of not guilty until False-peace is sent to the bar, and he denies the indictment, maintaining that he is not the accused person:

> If your Honours shall please to send for any that do intimately know me, or for the midwife that laid my mother of me, or for the Gossips that were at my Christning, they will any, or all of them prove that my name is not *False-peace* but *Peace*.

In seventeenth-century criminal law extreme precision was required in the wording of the indictment: a misnomer, or inaccurate naming or entitling of the prisoner, could enable the defence to plead that the whole indictment was invalid, so that the case could not proceed until a new bill had been drawn up.[8] Sir Matthew Hale's advice to Bunyan's wife had been to seek the release of her husband by means of a writ of error. Bunyan's hard-won legal experience provides him with a vehicle to express the power of sin to come unawares upon the soul, bearing a specious likeness to a duty or a harmless pastime. He can expose the mind's proneness to rationalize a sinful desire into something quite innocuous. The crier summons any in the court who can give information to stand forth, and a delightful legal pantomime ensues. Search-truth and Vouch-truth testify to having known the prisoner; Search-truth declares:

> My Lord, I know, and have known, this man from a child, and can attest that his name is *False-peace*. I knew his father, his name was *Mr. Flatter*, and his mother before she was married was called by the name of *Mrs. Soothup*. . . . I was his play-fellow only I was somewhat older than he; and when his mother did use to call him

home from his play, she used to say, *False-peace*, *False-peace*, come home quick or I'll fetch you. .... I can remember that when his mother did use to sit at the door with him, or did play with him in her arms, she would call him twenty times together, My little False-peace, my pretty False-peace. .... O my little bird False-peace; and how do I love my child. The gossips also know it is thus though he has had the face to deny it in open Court.

Moral argument, the "conceit" of the denial of the indictment, and an unfailing ear for common speech all blend together here, but the effortlessly true domestic interior is developed with such relish that it threatens to swallow up the other constituents. The evidence is damning, and False-peace is found guilty. A little later Pitiless pleads "Not guilty of pitilessness; all I did was to cheer-up according to my name, for my name is not Pitiless, but Cheer-up, and I could not abide to see Mansoul incline to melancholy". After the trial, there is the episode of the hiring fair when certain Diabolonians try to obtain employment in reformed Mansoul. Covetousness changes his name to Prudent Thrifty, and with him on market-day appear the Lord Lasciviousness and the Lord Anger, giving themselves out to be Harmless-mirth and Good-zeal respectively. "Three lusty fellows they were to look on and they were clothed in sheep's russet." Mr. Mind hires Prudent Thrifty, Mr. Godly-fear takes on Good-zeal, and the Lord Wilbewill makes Harmless-mirth his lackey, "because Lent was almost out".[9]

The common touch can be incongruous when it is found in situations which seem to demand, if not epic dignity, at least a less earthy flavour. In the days of Emanuel's triumph he gives a feast for the people of Mansoul, and entertains them with "some curious riddles of secrets"; both the vehicle and the meaning are of interest in this passage: the riddles are the Scriptures, which shows that Bunyan was ready to pay as much attention to figurative meanings as to the literal sense, and in the context illustrates the naïve audacity of his imagination. It is the quality which imparts charm to his emblem book, *A Book for Boys and Girls*; it is the child's freshness of vision, and it reappears, again alarmingly in the context of "Mansoul's wars", when the prince sends the chief men many "good bits" from his table, representing the scriptural promises of the new covenant.

The colloquial English of *The Holy War* is as muscular and racy as in any of the other major works, and does something to compensate for the thinness of characterization and the difficulties of the plot. There is actually more plain style and less sermon rhetoric than in *Badman* or *The Pilgrim's Progress*, because there are no pious dialogues between believers. Bunyan made a very few uneasy experiments with a kind of epic diction for his grand subject and then prudently abandoned them. The traces in the text are slight: Conscience has to preside over "all terrene and domestick matters". A hundred pages later Bunyan has forgotten the meaning of the exotic word "terrene", and writes about soldiers encamping before Eyegate, "in what terrene and terrible manner they could". Then there occur "dolorous notes", and "the profundity of your craft". He bears no stigma for indulging in these few extravagances; what is really remarkable is the natural soundness of judgement which prevents him from allowing any major adulteration of his style. For elsewhere the popular flavour is as strong as ever. A rumour spreads through the town "as a snowball loses nothing by rolling". Incredulity, describing the execution of his companions to Diabolus, says he would have "drunk of the same cup", if he had not escaped from the town. When Mr. Profane takes a secret message to Diabolus from his supporters in the town, he pauses at Hell-gate to gossip with Cerberus, and "they were presently as great as beggers". Mr. Carnal Security, who brings Mansoul "to dance after his Pipe", chides the more cautious citizens for their fear of being "sparrow-blasted". In most of these turns of phrase Bunyan has the benefit of the inventiveness of the folk; his own contribution is simply one of instinctive loyalty to the genius of his native speech. There are few similes which are not proverbs, or which, even if they are yet unrecorded from other sources, do not possess clear characteristics of the proverb, though their oral currency cannot be proved. It is as if all Bunyan's creativeness went into the larger imagery of his allegoric fable, and in language he was content to make use of what lay ready to his hand. Yet occasionally he can apply one of his images from common life

with original imaginative power. He sees the routed army of
the Doubters "spread upon the ground dead men, as one would
spread dung upon the land"; here we seem to see him reaching
once again towards epic seriousness and epic grimness. Clearly,
whether he had read Milton or not, literary epic would have
been no help to him. His style in this passage has more in
common with the terseness of *Beowulf* or the *Iliad*; but the
grimness is not sustained for long; comedy will keep breaking in.

IV

Bunyan, then, tries to grapple with his huge and awe-
inspiring subject by familiarizing it to himself and his readers
at every possible point and bringing it down to earth. He only
partly succeeds, because, while it is possible to apply this
treatment to the religious experience of humble people without
any distortion of essential truth, its application to heaven, hell
and eternity results in vulgarization; the parts of the book
directly concerned with Shaddai and Diabolus are inclined to
melodramatic sensation or to broad comedy. In the politics of
Mansoul, the partial success is achieved by describing what is
supposed in the allegory to be a powerful state as if it were a
small market town where everyone knew everyone else. A
great state trial is reported as if it were quarter sessions. In the
treatment of the war, and in everything pertaining to Emanuel's
army, where Bunyan is confronted with the most difficult
problems of his heroic theme, he also achieves partial success by
making the military detail contemporary. His method is regularly to exorcize the remote and alien by describing it in terms
of what he has seen and touched; if he has to visualize a mountain, he sets it down in a wide Bedfordshire field; and for his
battles and sieges he goes back to his own service in the county
levy.

The angelic hosts are drawn, not from the raw militia to
which he belonged, but from the regular regiments of the
New Model army. Like Cromwell's Ironsides, Emanuel's
officers can preach as well as fight; Captain Boanerges makes
Mansoul tremble with his sermon on the text, "Cut it down,

why cumbreth it the ground", for the barren fig-tree was a classic Puritan illustration of the depravity of the soul which could produce no fruits of grace.[10] Ill-Pause and Incredulity scoff at these captains as cavaliers might have done at sectarian soldiers who were also lay preachers; to them they are "Some Vagabond Runagate Crew . . . gotten together in tumultuous manner". Shaddai's first expeditionary force holds a prayer-meeting, just in the manner of the Ironsides, and has the same excellent comportment towards civilians that won the praise of Richard Baxter, for they pass "through the regions and countries of many people, not hurting or abusing any, but blessing wher-ever they come". The colours and scutcheons of the captains are minutely described, and may seem to be emblematic rather than realistic. They contain scriptural images: thus, Captain Conviction has for his device the book of the law wide open and his colours are pale; Captain Judgement has a burning fiery furnace and bears the red colours; and Captain Execution has a barren tree with an axe laid to its root. We learn however from Sir Charles Firth that in the Parliamentary army each company of foot or troop of horse had its distinguishing standard. Some captains had elaborate emblematical designs, such as a soldier with his sword drawn threatening a kneeling bishop![11]

There are innumerable other parallels with the conditions of the Civil War. Pikemen and musketeers are mentioned (the soldiers in the frontispiece are wearing contemporary dress and carrying pikes). Trumpeters are sent with messages. Prywell is given the post of Scoutmaster-general, an office peculiar to the English army. Technical terms are frequent. The "great guns" of Shaddai's army are the demi-culverins, firing a ball which weighed from sixteen to twenty pounds;[12] and the "Reformades" who ride with him are volunteer officers not attached to any particular formation.

Quite apart from Bunyan's personal and nostalgic interest in the regiments of the good old cause, he shares with his age an acceptance of the analogy between military order and the pattern of cosmic value, which is now entirely foreign to us, though a modest attempt to revive it may be detected in the later pages of Mr. Evelyn Waugh. For the seventeenth century, the virtues were above all orderly, moving to the honourable

discipline of arms. Milton's angels change guard in Eden in the
fourth book of *Paradise Lost*, and Marvell sees even the beauties
of nature in Fairfax's garden all the better for a little drill:

> See how the Flow'rs, as at Parade,
> Under their Colours stand displaid:
> Each Regiment in order grows,
> That of the Tulip, Pinke, and Rose.[13]

Bunyan's use of the military metaphor reflects the same conception of order overcoming chaos, but his realistic detail is
the vehicle for a more personal sentiment. Through the analogy
of the hosts of Emanuel and the Parliamentary regiments
he comes as near as ever he can in *The Holy War* to realizing
his theological subject-matter in a personal myth. The theme of
the army of the saints is interwoven with the theme of millenarian hope, which again takes Bunyan's mind back to the days
of the war and the Commonwealth, when that hope seemed
likely to be fulfilled. Looking backwards and forwards he sees
in the past, behind the years of betrayal and persecution, the
godly troops of the good old cause, in the future the army of
the saints who are to reign in splendour for a thousand years.
The pulse of this emotion can be felt in the description of the
drill of Emanuel's troops, which must recall field-days he had
witnessed at Newport Pagnell:

> They marched, they counter-marched, they opened to the
> right and left, they divided, and subdivided, they closed, they
> wheeled, made good their front and rear with their right and
> left wings, and twenty things more, with that aptness, and then
> were all as they were again, that they took, yea ravished the
> hearts that were in Mansoul to behold it. But add to this, the
> handling of their arms, the managing of their weapons of war,
> were marvellous taking to Mansoul and me.

The Holy War is indeed a magnificent failure, and, while it is
rich in ingenuity and observation, its most deeply felt parts take
us back into the mental hiding-places of Bunyan's past.

NOTES

CHAPTER VI

1. For Prudentius, see C. S. Lewis, *The Allegory of Love* (1936), pp. 66–73. Personified virtues and vices and the siege allegory in the middle ages are discussed in the chapter on allegory in G. R. Owst, *Literature and the Pulpit in Medieval England* (Cambridge, 1933). The following extract, from a Gloucester Cathedral MS., shows the traditional character of Bunyan's fable (the soul is speaking):
"(I am) besieged all about by the devil and his knights, but defended by the virtuous weapons that God hath given me . . . God himself is my constable and my defender" (Owst, p. 109).

2. *A Treatise of the Fear of God, Works*, ed. Offor, I, pp. 488–9.

3. The head of Bunyan, like the sleeping portrait prefixed to the third edition of *The Pilgrim's Progress*, was engraved by Robert White; both are based on a pencil drawing by the same artist, now in the Cracherode Collection in the British Museum.

4. Benjamin Keach, also a Baptist, and Bunyan's rival as a popular religious writer, had also described the debate of the fallen angels in *The Glorious Lover* (1679), pp. 190 ff.

Some lines in the prefatory verse to *The Holy War* suggest that Bunyan had looked at or heard about *Leviathan*, and John Wilkins's *Discovery of a New World in the Moon* (1668).

5. Cf. "And before I came to my Brothers, my Soul was made like the Chariotts of Aminnadab, and I was wounderfully bourne upp" (*Narrative of Agnes Beaumont*, p. 77).

6. *Exposition on the First Ten Chapters of Genesis, Works*, ed. Offor, II, p. 466.

The whole work is full of similar "typological" exegesis, in which everything is seen to anticipate some doctrine or incident in the life of Christ. The open-communion Baptist, Henry Jessey, admits the validity of multifold interpretation in certain passages, though he holds that "the literal sense of the matter and words is alwaies first to be taken" (*Miscellanea Sacra: or, Divers necessary Truths*, 1665, p. 16, "Rules about the Literal and Mystical Sense").

7. Brown, *John Bunyan*, pp. 316–18.

8. See Holdsworth, *History of English Law*, III (1923), pp. 614–31; and Blackstone, *Commentaries on the Laws of England* (1766–9), IV, pp. 301, 328.

9. The change of names on the part of the vices belongs to the morality tradition and reappears often in Puritan literature; it is found in Skelton's *Magnificence*, and in the Leveller Richard Overton's *Arraignment of Mr. Persecution* (1645) the villain gives his name in court as Present Reformation. See "The Trial of Vices in Puritan Fiction", *Baptist Quarterly*, Vol. XIV (January 1951), pp. 3–12.

10. It is the subject of Bunyan's sermon, *The Barren Fig-tree* (*Works*, ed. Offor, III, pp. 561–85).

11. Sir Charles Firth, *Cromwell's Army* (1912), p. 45.

12. Firth, *op. cit.*, p. 150.

13. Marvell, "Upon Appleton House", *Poems*, ed. H. M. Margoliouth, I, p. 68.

CHRISTIANA'S PILGRIMAGE

I

THE Second Part of *The Pilgrim's Progress* is entirely different from the first, and the frequent references to Christian and his journey serve only to emphasize the gulf between the two books. Bunyan had travelled a long way from the passionate cry of Christian in his agony which echoes through the earlier work; as a busy pastor, and the "Messenger" or evangelist of a widely scattered confederacy of meetings, he was now more concerned with external problems of conduct and church discipline than with recounting the experience of his conversion. The tendency to turn a shrewd eye outwards on human behaviour is already apparent in the satirical studies of Part One; *Badman* is dominated by the new, realistic, socially conscious Bunyan, and though in *The Holy War* he returned to the allegory of the soul, the treatment follows the traditional lines of the psychomachia, only rarely recapturing the full inwardness of his earlier attempt. In the Second Part, in the place of the lonely figures of Christian and his companion, battling with demons or disputing with heretics, there is a bustling, and on the whole a cheerful picture, of the life of a separatist church. Calvinism begins with an extraordinary interest in the self and ends with a perhaps excessive attention to the affairs of other people. Bunyan has already moved some distance along the curve of this development; it was inevitable that the sect founded by converts to produce more holy individuals should, in mingling them together, produce a communal life of a new type: the inner purity so earnestly sought gives place, without any necessary hypocrisy, to the cultivation of certain outward marks of conformity to the type. Some of the new characters of the Second Part seem convincing likenesses of the Bedford "brethren" and "sisters", and have less of universal human nature in them than their predecessors; but though they are types of Puritan education, their naturalness of speech and demeanour, and their possession of joyfulness without smugness, effectually separate them from those philistines of a later day who were to incur Arnold's irony.

When he composed his Second Part Bunyan was more sensitive to criticism than he had previously been. *The Pilgrim's Progress* had had its least favourable reception from the more strait-laced Baptists. A certain T. S., who had already written some improving novelettes, published his own Second Part in 1682, in which he endeavoured to remedy the defects of the original; in his view Bunyan had unduly neglected church life and the sacraments; T. S. tried to make up for this, and to "deliver the whole in such serious and spiritual phrases that may prevent that lightness and laughter which the reading of some passages therein may occasion in some vain and frothy minds".[1] T. S. was also a General Baptist, and he found fault with Bunyan's stress on a particular call to salvation received by Christian. He was certainly a humourless prig, and his book is written in an effete and cushioned style, but if his premiss is granted, that *The Pilgrim's Progress* is merely a useful tract, he cannot be put down as stupid. There were many of the godly who felt like him about the dangerous freedom of fiction; to them, Bunyan's fancy and his boisterous humour were acceptable enough within the comfortable confines of the sermon, but seemed in the allegory to have everything too much their own way. Bunyan's prefaces habitually strike the note of apology, as did that of Richard Bernard before him, and in the verses prefixed to his own Second Part he enumerates a whole series of objections. Some say he laughs too loud, or some condemn his method as mere romance. He defends himself sturdily, and his courage is not only due to his immense success; he speaks with the novelist's sense of proprietorship over his creations, as he defends "my Pilgrim", "my Christiana", "my neighbour Mercy"; and he refers indignantly to the number of counterfeit sequels which had already appeared (as distinguished from T. S.'s honest attempt to improve on the book).

The success of the First Part, the spurious continuations,

and sectarian criticism, all had their influence on the shaping
of Part Two. The author's interest in his own creation came
first, but, as in *The Holy War*, he could not help being aware
of his new stature and responsibility as a writer with a public.
The change of tone is established at the start when he addresses
his readers as "Courteous Companions". The whole movement of the story is more leisurely. As Monsignor Knox has
remarked, "Christian goes on a pilgrimage, Christiana on a
walking tour".[2] Like most sequels, it is an antiquarian tour
in which memories of former greatness are recalled, and
proper respect is paid at the scenes of Christian's deeds.
With the passage of years Christian and Faithful have grown
in heroic stature, and everyone along the king's highway seems
to know about them; but now, when his wife Christiana goes
on pilgrimage, we say goodbye to the male world of existential
decisions and heroic martyrdom; the atmosphere becomes
feminine and practical, with scope for the more tender feelings,
and the pilgrim theme is ingeniously reconciled with the
necessities of rearing a family.

Women had played an important part in the Bedford church
since its early days; by 1683 their prestige was such that Bunyan
had to contend with a demand for separate women's prayer-
meetings. In *A Case of Conscience Resolved* he summarily
rejected this proposal; after this rebuff he may well have felt
that the devotion of the female members of his congregation
required some recognition. The zeal of these women illustrates
the general revival of church life which was taking place now
that persecution had been relaxed. Corporate worship flourished,
as may be seen from the *Church Book*, where a regular succession of meetings for prayer and breaking of bread is recorded
in the years 1682–3. Together with their increased attention
to the sacraments, the Bedford separatists now made an open
display of their liberal principles regarding inter-communion;
the link with Cokayne's independent congregation in London
was strengthened, and Sister Joan Cooke, who had gone from
Bedford to live in London, was given permission to join any
congregation she thought good "for her edification and the
furtherance of her faith".[3] Against this background it is not
surprising to find in the Second Part references to the distinc-

tive Baptist sacrament of immersion, an indirect defence of congregational singing in the hymns scattered throughout the narrative, and, in the attractive studies of various types of tender conscience, like Fearing and Feeble-mind, some extremely clever open-communion propaganda. The graver heresies and back-slidings are no longer at the centre of the stage; the emphasis has shifted from heroics because Bunyan himself and his contemporaries were entering a less heroic age. If any single phrase illuminates the atmosphere of the Second Part as Christian's "What shall I do to be saved?" does the First, it is perhaps Christiana's "Bowels (i.e. pity, tenderness) becometh Pilgrims". We enter a more humdrum world, but a gracious and good-humoured one.

II

Bunyan makes a curious false start, but with his usual confidence he soon corrects himself and proceeds as if nothing had happened. After describing how, when released at last from multiplicity of business, he dreamed again in order to find out what had happened to Christiana and her children, he meets in his dream a Mr. Sagacity who begins to tell him the news from the city of Destruction. So here is a dream which is not a dream-vision at all, but simply a means of introducing a gossipy story in dialogue form like *Badman*:

> Better and better, quoth I. But what! Wife and Children and all? SAG. 'Tis true, I can give you an account of the matter, for I was upon the spot at the instant, and was thoroughly acquainted with the whole affair.

Sagacity is obviously a near relative of Wiseman, and the reader may well be daunted at the prospect of a pilgrimage recounted at second-hand by him. Bunyan's story-teller's instinct prompts him to drop Sagacity with a disarming naïveté, when he has related Christiana's journey as far as the Wicket-gate. "And now," he says, "Mr. *Sagacity* left me to Dream out my Dream by my self." Already his imagination has broken through the restraints of the dialogue form in the description of

Christiana's neighbours; reported speech gives way to direct
speech, so that he is involved in a dialogue within a dialogue.
Nothing could show more clearly that Bunyan worked without
any critical understanding of the potentialities of the various
narrative forms he employed. He simply took over conventional
devices like the dialogue and the dream-vision, and at this
point some suspension of his natural sense of what was fitting
allowed him to jumble them together. But at the Wicket-gate
the spell of his own fable fell upon him again; it was, after all,
the little door in the mountain of his old Elstow dream, when
he had thought the elect were in the sunshine on the other side;
at this moment the visual imagination takes full control.
Sagacity is abandoned, not because Bunyan's intelligence
informs him that immediacy is the essence of a dream narration,
but because he can now see without him.

From the start the theological outlines of the story are
less firmly drawn than in the First Part, for Christiana remains
a woman and the mother of a family, and does not submerge her
personality in the experience of conversion as Christian does.
Bunyan would probably have accepted

> He for God only, she for God in him,

as a correct statement of the case. The result is however
to make Christiana human and interesting, if not quite
satisfactory as a Calvinist object-lesson. Her repentance
begins with natural sorrow for her husband, "and for
that the loving bond of that Relation was utterly broken
betwixt them". Though she goes on to repent of her
sins, the thought which most wounds her conscience is
that she has in the past been disloyal to Christian and mis-
understood him. She does, indeed, receive her particular call
from God, in the form of a letter from the king, smelling "all of
the best Perfume", and is instructed to enter the road by the
Wicket-gate, but her assurance of grace is also an assurance that
it is her duty to rejoin her husband in heaven. When she and her
four boys are joined by a younger woman, Mercy, there is
the same emphasis on human affection as an incentive to the
awakening of the soul: Mercy's love for her friend comes first:

First, her Bowels yearned over *Christiana*: so she said with in herself, If my neighbour will needs be gone, I will go a little way with her, and help her. Secondly, her Bowels yearned ove. her own Soul (for what *Christiana* had said, had taken some hold upon her mind).

Furthermore she is assured by Christiana that she will not be rejected, even if she goes on pilgrimage only at her invitation. She sets off without any roll of election, and stands for a while outside the Gate while Christiana is admitted by the Keeper; she knocks loudly (Bunyan employs the Gospel metaphor for fervent prayer) and is received just as she is falling into a swoon. The Keeper of the Gate takes her gently in, reminding her that he prays for all who believe in him, "by what means soever they come unto me"; and Bunyan calls special attention to these words by a "mark this" in the margin.

Clearly the strict letter of Calvinist orthodoxy has been deliberately compromised in order to appease the conscience of those who were inclined to enter the holy community on account of the ties of friendship or kindred, and whose religious convictions, however genuine, did not find expression in a twice-born conversion of the old violent kind. Later, in the Interpreter's House, Mercy is told that she is in the way of salvation because she has given credit to the truth in the person of Christiana; like Ruth she has left home and parents "for the love that she bore to Naomi and to the Lord her God". The Keeper of the Gate who is so tender to Mercy is Christ; his presence, embodying mercy and forgiveness, is much more in evidence than in the parallel episode in Part One, where Christian is admitted by a vague figure called Good Will.

The pilgrims have already been frightened by the devil's dog before reaching the Gate. Now, as they walk along by the wall past the devil's orchard, they are assaulted by two "ill-favoured ones" who are the demons beheld by Christiana in her former dreams. Meanwhile her boys have eaten some of the fruit from the overhanging orchard trees, and this is to have troublesome consequences later. The women are rescued by the Reliever, who promises that he will ask their Lord to send them a conductor. One by one the familiar stages of the pilgrimage are revisited, and the first is the Interpreter's House. There are some fresh emblem pictures for the inspection of Christiana's party; and also an addition to the house calculated to have a special appeal to Baptists—a Bath of Sanctification. There is no reference in the earlier version of the episode to the sacrament of baptism by immersion; however, though a concession is now made to sectarian feeling, Bunyan does not give pride of place to the symbolic bath; he simply remarks that his pilgrims were strengthened as well as purified by it, and that "when they came in they looked fairer a deal, then when they went out to the washing". Also Christiana gives a summary of her religious experience to the Interpreter, just as new converts at Bedford meeting were required to do in the presence of the minister and the whole church.

When the women leave the house of the Interpreter, they are accompanied by a guide and protector, Greatheart. It is Great-heart, not Christiana, who is the real successor to Christian in Part Two; both are projections of the author's personality: Christian exhibits in his character the miseries and splendours of conversion, while Greatheart represents Bunyan in the role of pastor. His self-portrait has become that of a calm, determined knight of the faith, free from all the sickly fears which had once oppressed him. As Christiana and her family move on their way towards the Hill Difficulty, Greatheart lectures to them on the nature of special grace, just as Bunyan must have exhorted his congregation.

Everywhere are memorials of Christian's journey, so that the atmosphere is more like that of a peace-time tour of the battlefields than of a new campaign. They pass by Simple, Sloth and Presumption, hanging in irons at the side of the highway. The by-ways which Formality and Hypocrisy took have been walled off. Indeed many of the rigours of pilgrimage seem to have been softened for their benefit. Hill Difficulty puts them "in a pelting heat", but is no more troublesome than that. Outside the Palace Beautiful there is, as well as the lions, a giant called Grim or Bloody-man, who stands in the allegory for the persecutions of the civil power (he is a relative of the Blood-men) but he is soon dispatched by Greatheart. The House Beautiful is no longer a mere stage on the way where champions are refreshed before travelling on to fresh combats; on this more leisured pilgrimage it becomes a symbol of the communal life of the church, seen now not simply as a preparation for the individual's spiritual warfare (as Bunyan had treated his earliest contacts with Gifford's small gathering) but as a good in itself. Christiana and her family stay over a month, entertained by Providence and Charity and the other female virtues.

These Puritan maidens instruct the little boys in their catechism, while Mercy is courted by the worldly Mr. Brisk.[4] It is hard to see what he is doing in the House Beautiful; clearly, Bunyan is drifting once again from the world of allegory towards the sphere of realistic social observation as he had practised it in *Badman*. He turns again to the problem of marriage with unbelievers, and shows Mercy behaving as Badman's unfortunate wife ought to have done. She is easily able to rid herself of her unwelcome suitor by telling him that the needlework at which she is always busy is not for herself but for the poor. Mr. Brisk sees her as no longer a good housewife but as one "troubled with ill conditions". Mercy does not let her piety prevent her from having a proper pride in her own good looks, and her concession to human weakness in the episode shows her in an altogether natural and charming light:

I might a had Husbands afore now, tho' I spake not of it to any; but they were such as did not like my Conditions, tho' never did any of them find fault with my Person. So they and I could not agree.

These touches of nature are always breaking through to relieve the monotony of exemplary conduct. The little boy James will give an answer which may seem to savour of priggishness in one so young, if he did not blush deeply when Greatheart compliments him for it. Bunyan is creating his characters now from a direct study of good little boys and virtuous girls with all their human limitations, while he avails himself rather less frequently of the pure allegorical principle.

As a corollary of this progress towards pure fiction, when the allegory is applied, its association with the story tends to be arbitrary and somewhat insensitively conceived. This is

K

shown in the next episode, when Matthew's stomach begins to
suffer from the fruit he has eaten in the devil's garden. Mr.
Skill, the doctor, is called, and he gives him pills compounded
ex Carne et Sanguine Christi, which bring about a violent
purge "and did quite rid him of his Gripes". The picture of
Matthew writhing with indigestion, "pulled as 'twere both
ends together", and of his mother persuading him to take the
pill by touching it with the tip of her tongue, is certainly not
the most decorous comment on the nature of original sin. But
it is an amusing domestic interior in the Dutch fashion, recalling
some of the earthier anecdotes in Bunyan's sermons; and to
complain of bad taste is beside the point, for it is part of the
almost medieval simplicity of his religious outlook to indulge
in broad humour about the fundamentals of his faith. There was
still an audience to appreciate such humour, though some even
among his fellow-Nonconformists were beginning to apply the
new standard of propriety which indicates the modern fragmen-
tated mind. There is even a pun on the name of a well-known
universal remedy of the Restoration period, Mathew's powders,
which attained a reputation commensurate with that of some
modern proprietary medicines.[5]

Other graces of life, as well as humour, are present in
good measure on Christiana's pilgrimage. Bunyan's love of music
is revealed in the entertainment made for Christiana and Mercy
when they have retired to their room in the House Beautiful.
There is a certain mystery about it, for we hear of it only
through the women's conversation. "Wonderful!" says Christiana, "Musick in the House, Musick in the Heart, and Musick
also in Heaven, for joy that we are here." Bunyan is near
enough to the old order to accept unconsciously the analogy of
music and moral harmony. As they leave the house the birds
in the grove sing to them from Sternhold's version of the Psalms;
and later the different temperaments of Christians are compared to the qualities of different musical instruments: diffident
professors like Mr. Fearing are likened to the sackbut (a kind of
trombone) whose notes are more doleful than those of other
instruments.

The Valley of Humiliation and the Valley of the Shadow of
Death have lost many of their terrors, and the passage of the

travellers through them is something of an anti-climax. The women find the first valley a beautiful tract of rich meadow-ground; here in an atmosphere of almost pastoral ease a shepherd-boy sings to them a song smoother and more lyrically sweet than Bunyan's verses customarily are:

> I am content with what I have
> Little be it, or much:
> And, Lord, contentment still I crave,
> Because thou savest such.

> Fulness to such a burden is
> That go on Pilgrimage:
> Here little, and hereafter Bliss,
> Is best from Age to Age.

It is because the women possess their share of Christian humility that they have no Apollyon to oppose them. Christian, they are told, had to pay for the few slips he had when going down the hill: that is to say, he was not so successful in the practice of humility. Bunyan is frankly admitting a tendency to pride as his own peculiar failing. Had he not acknowledged this temptation in his autobiography where he speaks of "pride and liftings up of Heart" as a constant thorn in the flesh to him? Even in his last years his friend George Cokayne admitted that he needed to keep a tight rein upon this weakness lest he should be "exalted above measure". [6]

The small boy Samuel wants to know all about his father's fight with Apollyon. There is actually a monument with an inscription when they come to the place, and all around are tokens of the heroic struggle: blood-stains on the stones, dints upon the ground, and some shivers of the demon's broken darts.

The Valley of the Shadow is longer and more terrible to them. There are groanings and shakings of the ground, and demons and lions which disappear when, under Greatheart's protection and encouragement, they advance unflinchingly. Even for the women and children there must be some heart-searching; the torments of introspective doubt are not wholly remitted, but, unlike Christian, they have their pastor at their elbow, urging and exhorting them.

At the end of the valley, where Christian had found Giant Pope in his cave, impotently sitting and biting his nails, their way is barred by another giant named Maul. Immediately before the Popish Plot the Roman Catholic church seemed to Bunyan and his fellow-Protestants a weak and distant enemy. In 1684, after the alarums of the Plot and the Exclusion Bill controversy, the Roman power had become once again the chief menace to the Gospel. Maul is a revived version of Giant Pope; he "did use to spoil young Pilgrims with Sophistry", an accusation commonly brought against the Jesuits, who had figured extensively in the depositions concerning the plot. There is a desperate fight before Greatheart finally cuts off the giant's head; it is a combat conducted according to the approved conventions of popular romance: at one point the champion is beaten to his knees, and half way through there is, by tacit consent, a respite for the combatants to draw breath.

As the pilgrims proceed, they are joined by other wayfarers. There are long conversations and long halts, until the leisurely progress becomes a delightful ramble through a country from which most of the dangers have been removed. The most vividly conceived of the newcomers is Old Honest, whom they come upon asleep under an oak tree, and who hastens up to defend himself, thinking they are footpads. "Not Honesty in the *abstract*, but *Honest* is my Name," he says, and the remoteness of Bunyan's living, breathing characters from mere moral abstractions could not be better put. In Honest, even the idea so common in Christian allegory, as in Spenser, of a human being striving towards the attainment of a particular virtue, is not forced upon our attention; he is equally compounded of modesty, integrity, and unassuming bravery; above all he is the veteran, a type now becoming dear to Bunyan, the tried and tested campaigner who does not waste words about his experiences. He introduces a manly, slightly more worldly atmosphere, into a book in which women have been so far predominant: even Greatheart is induced to greet him in a slangy way, as "a cock of the right kind", using the profane language of the cock-fight. Later he is joined by

Valiant-for-Truth, who has just repulsed three assailants single-handed, and speaks of his prowess in a manner that is almost swashbuckling:

> So we fell to it, one against three, for the space of above three Hours. They have left upon me, as you see, some of the Marks of their Valour, and have also carried away with them some of mine. . . . I fought till my Sword did cleave to my Hand; and when they were joined together, as if a Sword grew out of my Arm, and when the Blood run thorow my Fingers, then I fought with most Courage.

It may be allowed that much of this is symbolic; the sword is St. Paul's sword of the spirit, and the blood is that of Christ's atonement, but the doctrinal or scriptural emphasis of the marginal glosses cannot alter the impression made by the narrative. And here that impression, as in the case of Lord Wilbewill's return to his true allegiance, is of human dignity and courage.

The other later recruits to the band of pilgrims form a closely knit group in which a didactic intention is more clearly apparent. These are the sincere believers who are so tormented by difficulties and scruples that they cannot enter conscientiously into the full life of the church without very careful handling. There is Feeblemind, who does not like gay attire or unprofitable questions and admits that it is his weakness to be offended by that which others have a liberty to do. There is Fearing, who, like the Bunyan of *Grace Abounding*, is morbidly doubtful whether he will be accepted at last. Finally they are joined by Ready-to-halt, whose allegorical lameness might well symbolize the spiritual weakness of this whole group of over-scrupulous professors. But they all reach their goal and pass bravely through some tests of the religious life which daunt braver men: though Fearing thinks the hob-goblins will have him in the Valley of the Shadow, at Vanity Fair he is a very lion for courage. Above all, they are kindly entertained by Greatheart and Christiana's family. This is the chief lesson which Bunyan was anxious for the reader to draw from these characters: the gathered church should welcome all who were sound on the main points of doctrine, no matter how much they differed ov

minor scruples, and however small their contribution to the
social life of the holy community was likely to be. The need for
maintaining communion with such weak and feeble brethren is
explicitly mentioned in Bunyan's tract on church principles,
A Confession of my Faith,[7] and it was of course an essential
part of the tradition of Bedford meeting.

Another topic of controversial interest to Baptists which is
treated with an unobtrusive propagandist skill is church-
singing. Bunyan, himself a musician and a home-spun poet,
belonged like Benjamin Keach to the section of opinion which
was favourable to congregational singing. As well as including
quotations from the metrical version of the Psalms, the narrative is interspersed with original hymns. After the shepherd
boy's song there is the famous pilgrims' song, which is appro-
priately placed after Valiant-for-truth has given an account of
adventures:

> Who would true Valour see,
> Let him come hither;
> One here will constant be,
> Come Wind, come Weather.
>
> There's no Discouragement,
> Shall make him once Relent,
> His first avow'd Intent,
> To be a Pilgrim.

The hymn has become widely known far outside Baptist
congregations; in it Bunyan attains a bold simplicity free from
the slightest trace of doggerel. Some of the words and rhymes
seem like echoes from Amiens' song in *As You Like It*; but had
Bunyan read Shakespeare?[8]

The rest of the journey can be briefly summarized though
progress seems slower than ever in the later stages. They put
up at the inn of one Gaius and stay there more than a month.
Gaius provides an illustration of the curious manner in which
the Bible acts as an influence on the form of the episodes and the
allegorical properties they contain; the debt to Scriptural
texts, often very literally and crudely interpreted, for the
shaping of the story, is considerable, and much more obvious

than any Biblical influences on prose style. Gaius is mentioned by St. Paul in the Authorized Version of the *Epistle to the Romans* as "mine host, and of the whole church", so Bunyan makes him an innkeeper. There is welcome for pilgrims and a supper with various allegorical dishes. After supper Honest amuses the company by asking riddles. Divine riddles were among the Prince's entertainments for his people in *The Holy War*. The riddle is a poor relation of the emblem, that literary form so much admired by Bunyan, and in his last years he was working, as we have seen, on an emblem book of his own, *A Book for Boys and Girls*.

The time-scheme of the pilgrimage is treated more elastic- ally than even the leisureliness and the long halts can justify. Mercy is now married to Matthew, who only a short time before was a naughty boy robbing orchards; and Christiana is des- cribed as "an aged Matron", which seems totally at variance with the impression made by her words and carriage elsewhere. Before their departure James is married to Gaius' daughter Phoebe; and, on the eve of their setting out, the men go upon what can only be described as a giant-hunt. Gaius has a giant, Slay-good, on his land, and invites the others to rid the country of him in a manner which suggests a proposal for a day's shooting: "Since Mr. Greatheart is good at his Weapons, if you please, after we have refreshed ourselves, we will walk into the Fields, to see if we can do any good." The monsters, in Part Two, have been banished to the outskirts of the story; they are the source of fairy-tale entertainment, no longer of real spiritual terror.

Gaius makes an eloquent compliment to the women, in order to take away the reproach of Eve, and to testify to their real contemporary importance in the gathered churches. It was women who followed Christ, a woman who washed his feet with tears, women who sat by the sepulchre and brought the first tidings that he was risen: "Women therefore are highly favoured, and shew by these things that they are sharers with us in the Grace of Life."

At Vanity Fair the whole company are entertained by Mr. Mnason, another host of the apostles (Acts xxi, 16). Things have changed much at the fair, and there are many other believers staying at the house. As at the other places of resort, everybody knows about Christiana:

> Who do you think this is? ... It is *Christiana*, the Wife of *Christian*, that famous Pilgrim, who with *Faithful* his Brother were so shamefully handled in our Town.

Instead of persecution there is a continuation of the social, gossipy existence they have been leading at the other hostels along the route; there are good people in this reformed Vanity Fair who do not seem to be going on pilgrimage at all. This is a reflection of the easier conditions for Nonconformists since the First Part had been written; however, the confusion of the allegory thus caused provides an unconscious statement of the change in religious viewpoint between the two parts. The earlier pilgrims are moving to a goal; their dynamic creed makes every part of life a preparation, a hindrance, or a test. Christiana and her family saunter towards the promised land, but they might just as well settle down with their husbands at Mr. Mnason's or at Gaius' inn, and live the good life there. They are the second generation in whom Christianity has permeated every aspect of the common life, so that, paradoxically, for them the world and the flesh are no longer shocking. There is music, dancing and humour; Ready-to-halt casts aside his crutches (another unfortunate allegorical slip, since they were "the Promises"); and Mercy is made the subject of the old joke about the longings of pregnancy, so common in seventeenth-century comedy: she longs for the Shepherds' marvellous glass and her mother-in-law prevails on them to give it to her. By this time the atmosphere of this world which is being made safe for Puritanism has become so compelling that we are not surprised when Greatheart organizes an expedition against Doubting Castle and slays Giant Despair. The spectres of *Grace Abounding* have indeed been laid.

But Bunyan, with one of those strokes of art that are more apparent in the Second Part than in the First, has kept his major statement of the heroic splendours of belief until the last. The pilgrims cross the river of death in one of the greatest passages of his prose, and one of the few which is a consciously ordered set piece. The adagio movement of what has gone before throws it into bold relief. As one by one the pilgrims receive the summons to join their prince across the river, a formalized pattern is repeated with variations: the formula consists of the invitation, an emblematic token of the truth of the message, the bequests of the dying man to his friends, and his last words when crossing the river. Most of the tokens are drawn from the imagery of the twelfth chapter of Ecclesiastes: they include the golden bowl, the pitcher broken at the well, and the wheel broken at the cistern; the text was employed thus in ministerial biographies as a commentary on physical dissolution, and it looks as if it may have become an established convention of death-bed scenes.[9] Through the conventional pattern the noble assertions of Valiant-for-truth and his companions stand out. "*My Sword*, I give to him that shall succeed me in my Pilgrimage, and my *Courage* and *Skill*, to him that can get it." The boast contains a grand contempt for theological niceties.

The Second Part of *The Pilgrim's Progress* is an interesting commentary on the capacity of middle age, whether in an individual or a community, to reduce an overwhelming spiritual experience to more manageable proportions. Its expository skill, and the liveliness of its scenes and characters are admirable; there is a more conscious manipulation of people and incidents by the author, in the direction of humour and humanity. We may feel

Behold, the visionary splendour fades,

but it is not the shades of night which approach, but a cheerful daytime world; and everywhere in this world there are memories and traces of the past; the dynamic experience of Christian casts its long shadow.

L

NOTES

CHAPTER VII

1. T. S., *The Second Part of the Pilgrim's Progress*, The Author's Apology.

2. Ronald A. Knox, *Essays in Satire* (1928), p. 206.

3. *Church Book*, p. 71, 30th March, 1682.

4. "Brisk" could carry a bad sense in the late seventeenth century, and mean rather flashy or "fast". The *N.E.D.* quotes Etheredge, *Man of Mode*: "He has been, as the sparkish word is, Brisk Upon the Ladies already."

5. See Richard Mathew, *The Unlearned Alchymist His Antidote, or, A more full and ample Explanation of the Use, Virtue and Benefit of my PILL* (1662). Mathew's pills were "a corrector of all Vegetative poysons", and like those in the story had to be taken in a liquid (pp. 107, 109).

6. "A Preface to the Reader" in Bunyan's *Acceptable Sacrifice*, Offor, *Works*, I, p. 685.

7. Offor, *Works*, II, p. 610.

8. *The Pilgrim's Progress*, ed. E. Venables (Oxford, 1900), p. 480.

9. "About a week before he died, when his silver cord began to loosen, and his golden bowle to breake . . ." Edward Bagshaw, *Life and Death of Mr. Bolton*, 3rd ed. 1635 p. 32.

CHAPTER VIII

CONCLUSION

The Pilgrim's Progress is of the rare number of books which will always have readers, whether the pundits of literary taste should approve of it or not. It has, in fact, achieved an existence that is independent of literature; for the literary quality of a book is commonly weakened when it is translated into another language, but Bunyan's allegory has been translated into literally hundreds of dialects, and has maintained its appeal as a universal religious myth. From the early nineteenth century onwards, the activity of foreign missions in Africa, Asia and Oceania, made the book available in cheap editions as a missionary tract, and the process is still going on. The sophisticated Western reader will accept even a bad translation of a book about which he feels he ought to know something. More primitive peoples start with no such prepossessions, and yet the allegory has made its way among them. The conclusion seems to be that, when all due allowance has been made for the beauty of the English words in which Bunyan has clothed his fable, his supreme achievement lies in the dream itself: the archetypal figures of the pilgrim, the burden, the monsters, the road with its sloughs and by-paths, the guides true and false, the gentle hospitality at the places of resort, and the final bourne of the heavenly city across the river, all these call up similar profound, though not easily definable, responses, in readers belonging to widely separated cultural traditions.

If one turns over a number of these missionary versions of *The Pilgrim's Progress*, one is struck by the apparent incongruity of the illustrations to be found in many of the editions. Here in one is Christian equipped like a medieval Chinese warrior and Apollyon in the shape of a Chinese dragon. In another, designed for a racial group in the Malay Archipelago, some mid-Victorian engravings have been reproduced; as we contemplate the late romantic landscapes, the idealized Puritan maidens, the abundant lace and steeple-crowned hats, now made available to those who can follow the story in Sea-Dyak, our sense that this is just another instance of cultural confusion in a world bedevilled by the facility of its communications, gives place to a realization that all these particular trappings of time and place are irrelevant to the kind of communication that is taking place. The illustrations, whether their style is strange or familiar, serve only to present, as it were, the Platonic ideas of a warrior, an evil monster, a comforting female presence.

But to a far smaller group of people Bunyan means much more than this. In the Anglo-Saxon countries his myth of the pilgrim is inseparable from the sturdy and simple English in which it is related; and it is also inevitably associated with the Puritan tradition for which it provides a classic expression. While the Christian tradition was taken for granted, so was *The Pilgrim's Progress*. Until the second quarter of the nineteenth century it was generally regarded as a popular religious manual which happened to be admirably written; thus we find an underground current of praise for it in chance remarks thrown off by men of letters, including Swift, Richardson and Johnson; it was not considered as polite literature, for it belonged to an entirely different sphere. During the changes caused by the romantic movement, all this was altered. Bunyan was acclaimed as a type of the natural genius, and in the revaluation of literature then in progress he was placed alongside Homer, Burns and the writers of the ballads. The John Murray edition of 1830 was the first Bunyan for highly educated people; it had Southey's famous introduction and two sensational engravings by John Martin: the tinker had reached the intellectuals. Of course much in the romantic appraisement of Bunyan is true, and needed to be done; the romantics' theory of poetry enabled them to appreciate the deeper nature of the creative process and its relation to the myth-making faculty of the unconscious mind; standing on their shoulders, it is easier for us to recognize that primary mythical appeal of the work which transcends most cultural barriers.

However, a less fortunate consequence of the nineteenth-century taste for Bunyan was the neglect of his historical background; the spotlight of an age of individualism was shone upon the sublime tinker, while the theology and the popular rhetoric he shared with countless other field-preachers were left in a surrounding darkness. The scholarship of the last half century has done much to illuminate this darkness; the study of the development of Puritan literary genres has shown how much traditional material was at Bunyan's disposal, as well as his Bible. Yet now that he can be studied as a sectary among the sectaries, his individual stature is not at all diminished. One has only to examine the allegorical tracts of his rival, Benjamin Keach, to realize the unbridgeable gap between original genius and pedestrian application, even when the same literary form and the same subject is treated by either writer, and when Bunyan is just as limited by didactic intention as his fellow-Baptist. In fact, Bunyan, like any writer of importance, provides a study in the interaction of tradition and the individual talent. His place at the end of the succession of popular homiletic writing, stretching from the middle ages to Dent and the Puritan preachers, is assured; so is his anticipation—one might almost say his unwilling anticipation—of much in the bourgeois novel, in Defoe, and later in Dickens: the satire, the domestic humour, the names and the characters drawn from one predominant trait, all recur. But these are the bloodless affinities of literary history: his originality lies in the power which enabled him to project his visions and obsessions on to the objective reality of a work of art: to turn *Grace Abounding* into *The Pilgrim's Progress*.

BIBLIOGRAPHY

(i) WORKS BY BUNYAN

The Works of Mr. John Bunyan, ed. John Doe (1692)
This edition in one-volume folio, by a printer who had known Bunyan, is incomplete.

The Works of John Bunyan, ed. George Offor (3 vols., London and Edinburgh, 1860–2)
The extensive commentary is Evangelical rather than scholarly, but this is the last complete edition, containing all the minor works and sermons.

The Pilgrim's Progress, 2nd ed., ed. J. B. Wharey, revised by Roger Sharrock (Oxford, Clarendon Press, 1960)

Grace Abounding to the Chief of Sinners, ed. Roger Sharrock (Oxford, Clarendon Press, 1962)

Grace Abounding and The Pilgrim's Progress, ed. Roger Sharrock (Oxford Standard Authors, O.U.P., 1966)

The Holy War and *The Life and Death of Mr. Badman*, ed. John Brown (Cambridge English Classics, C.U.P., 1905)

The Life and Death of Mr. Badman, ed. G. B. Harrison (World's Classics, O.U.P., 1929)

God's Knotty Log, ed. Henri A. Talon (Meridian Books, New York, 1961)
A paperback edition of *The Pilgrim's Progress* which incorporates *The Heavenly Footman* as a specimen of Bunyan's non-allegorical homiletic writing.

(ii) THE PURITAN BACKGROUND

Baxter, Richard. *Reliquiae Baxterianae* (1696; reprinted in Dent's Everyman's Library)

The Narrative of the Persecution of Agnes Beaumont in 1674, ed. with an Introduction by G. B. Harrison (Constable's Miscellany, 1929)

Calamy Revised, ed. A. G. Matthews (O.U.P., 1934)

The Journeys of Celia Fiennes, ed. Christopher Morris (Cresset Press, 1947)

Fox, George. *Journal*, revised ed. by John Nickalls (C.U.P., 1952)

Hutchinson, Lucy. *Memoirs of Colonel Hutchinson* (Dent's Everyman's Library)

Morgan, Joseph. *History of the Kingdom of Basaruah*, ed. R. B. Schlatter (Harvard U.P., 1946)

The Puritans, ed. Perry Miller and T. H. Johnson (American Book Co., New York, 1938)
  A useful collection of texts.

(iii) MODERN STUDIES

(a) *Historical and Theological*

Barclay, Robert. *The Inner Life of the Religious Societies of the Commonwealth* (1876)

Brown, L. F. *Baptists and Fifth Monarchy Men during the Interregnum* (O.U.P., 1912)

Dowden, Edward. *Puritan and Anglican* (Paul, 1900)

Haller, William. *The Rise of Puritanism* (Columbia U.P., 1938)

Haller, William. *Liberty and Reformation in the Puritan Revolution* (Columbia U.P., 1953)

Nuttall, Geoffrey F. *The Holy Spirit in Puritan Faith and Experience* (Blackwell, 1946)

Paul, Robert S. *The Lord Protector: Religion and Politics in the Life of Oliver Cromwell* (Lutterworth Press, 1955)

Schenk, Wilhelm. *The Concern for Social Justice in the Puritan Revolution* (Longmans, 1948)

Tawney, R. H. *Religion and the Rise of Capitalism* (Murray, 1926)

Troeltsch, Ernest. *The Social Teaching of the Christian Churches*, trans. Olive Wyon (Allen & Unwin, 1931)

Whiting, C. E. *Studies in English Puritanism, 1660–1688* (S.P.C.K., 1931)

(b) *Biographical and Literary*

Blondel, Jacques. *Allégorie et réalisme dans le Pilgrim's Progress* (Archives des Lettres Modernes, 1959)

Brown, John. *John Bunyan, His Life, Times and Work* (1885; revised by F. M. Harrison, Hulbert Publishing Co., 1928)

Firth, Sir Charles. *Essays Historical and Literary* (O.U.P., 1938)

Frye, R. M. *God, Man and Satan* (Princeton, 1960)

Godber, Joyce. 'The Imprisonments of John Bunyan' in *Transactions of the Congregational Historical Society*, xvi (1949)

Grierson, Sir Herbert. *Cross Currents in English Literature of the Seventeenth Century* (Chatto & Windus, 1927)

Griffith, Gwilym O. *John Bunyan* (Hodder & Stoughton, 1927)

Harrison, F. M. *A Bibliography of the Works of John Bunyan* (Oxford, 1932; Supplement No. 6 to the *Transactions of the Bibliographical Society*)

Harrison, G. B. *John Bunyan: A Study in Personality* (Dent, 1928)

Hussey, Maurice. In Pelican Guide to English Literature, vol. iii: *From Donne to Marvell* (1956)

Iser, Wolfgang. *Bunyan's Pilgrmi's Progress: die kalvinistische Heilsgewissheit und die Form des Romans*, in *Festschrift fur Walther Bulst* (Heidelberg, 1960)

Kaufmann, U. M. *The Pilgrim's Progress and Traditions in Puritan Meditation* (New Haven, 1966)

Leavis, F. R. In *The Common Pursuit* (Chatto & Windus, 1952)

Rutherford, Mark (William Hale White). *John Bunyan* (1905; new ed., Nelson, 1933)

Sharrock, Roger. 'Personal Vision and Puritan Tradition in Bunyan', *Hibbert Journal* (1957)

Sharrock, Roger. *The Pilgrim's Progress* (Studies in English Literature 27; Arnold, 1966)

Shaw, George Bernard. In *Dramatic Opinions and Essays* (Constable, 1907) (from the Preface to *Man and Superman*)

Southey, Robert. Introduction to his edition of *The Pilgrim's Progress* (1830; reprinted in *Select Biographies*, 1844)

Talon, Henri A. *John Bunyan, the Man and his Works* (Rockliff, 1951)

Tindall, W. Y. *John Bunyan, Mechanick Preacher* (Columbia U.P., 1934)

Van Ghent, Dorothy. In *The English Novel: Form and Function* (Rinehart, 1953)

Wharey, J. B. *The Sources of Bunyan's Allegories* (J. H. Furst Co., Baltimore, 1904)

Winslow, O. L. *John Bunyan* (Macmillan Co., New York, 1961)

INDEX